everything
happens
for a
reason

Suzane Northrop

JODERE
GROUP
San Diego, California

everything
happens
for a
reason

Love, Free Will,
and the Lessons of the Soul

133.9 Nor

JODERE
G R O U P

JODERE GROUP, INC.
P.O. Box 910147
San Diego, CA 92191-0147
800.569.1002 • www.jodere.com

Book design by Charles McStravick

Editorial supervision by Chad Edwards

CIP data available from the Library of Congress

ISBN 1-58872-043-8

05 04 03 02   4 3 2 1
First printing, November 2002

PRINTED IN THE UNITED STATES OF AMERICA

I dedicate this book to

hazel katherine watson

and

dorothy e. edison,

my beloved grandmothers

contents

preface

There is one spectacle grander than the sea,
that is the sky;
There is one spectacle grander than the sky,
that is the interior of the soul.

— VICTOR HUGO

Whether it's repeating patterns that keep us on a negative course, or making choices that send us in a positive direction, whether it's thirsting for the understanding of why certain things happen, or struggling to resolve the issues of love and loss—virtually everything that occurs to challenge, support, or simply to change the way we live our life—happens for a reason. And the reason, while it may not be immediately clear to us, most often has to do with whatever lesson or lessons our souls need to learn so that we can move on to the next stage of our spiritual development.

As humans, we have always wanted to know the answers to our questions around life and death: Is there a God? Why is life so filled with chaos and pain? How can I achieve uninterrupted fulfillment in my life? Why are we here at all? Is there really life after death? Up until now, death has been the "Great Mystery."

Inevitably, we will all experience loss of a loved one at some point in our lives, and the nature of that loss—when it occurs, whom we lose, what our relationship with that person was like in life, and how we choose to address that loss—will determine the nature of our grief, and set the time frame for our grieving process. To live through the loss of a loved one is always a lesson in itself, and sometimes it's a lesson that can help to awaken us to the significance of many other aspects of our own life. Those who have passed over, the DPs as I lovingly call them, make themselves available to help us as they connect from the other side with their messages of love and support. But what we do with those messages is up to us. In almost every present moment we will find ourselves at a point of making a choice in our lives. Free will and choice are still ours.

The mission of our soul incarnating into human form is to elevate to a higher spiritual level. Thus, we have been given the divine gift of *free will* when it comes to the path we take here on Earth toward changing our ways and expanding the understanding of our spiritual selves. Attempting to live our lives in a way that is accountable and responsible is perhaps the most challenging task of all. We become masters at diverting ourselves by taking up causes, seeking out yet another new philosophy, or crusading to change the world instead of just looking inward and trying to change ourselves. It is too easy to hand the responsibility of learning the *Soul Lessons* of unconditional love, compassion, understanding, patience, and forgiveness over to another person, whether it be a loved one, teacher, or guru.

Make no mistake; those who are in your life now as well as those who have moved on have either been drawn to you, or you to them, to learn some kind of lesson. I would like for you to understand, as I do, that there are no coincidences. We are all here for a reason. We are not here by some random *roll of the dice* by the Universe. Each of us is part of one of the greatest "spiritual schools" offered for the evolution of the Soul. And with that in mind, every person, and situation—be they difficult, confusing, joyous, or enlightening—is present for a reason. We may not understand why today, tomorrow, or for a decade. All we have to know now is that whatever it is that we are going through, there is a reason attached to it. Rest assured that at some point we will always get an opportunity for understanding and insight, but not necessarily right away.

In *Everything Happens for a Reason*, I'll be talking about how the choices we make—before birth, during life, and after death—affect not only our own lives but also those of the people we love. I'll talk about how different kinds of death can affect the lives of those left behind, and how the DPs and the living can help one another to heal from the loss and move on. I'll discuss the ways in which those who've suffered similar losses—of a child, a sibling, a parent, or a close friend to disease, lengthy illness, suicide, tragedies, accidents, or natural causes—seem drawn together for learning and support by a bond of psychic energy I've seen demonstrated in my workshops and sessions, time and again. And, I will provide personal stories along the way that certain people have so graciously allowed me to share about their healing messages from the DPs to illustrate my points.

It is my wish for you, as you read this book that you walk away with an expanded understanding of life after death—the Afterlife—and how each soul creates its own program for learning the key disciplines. That you truly learn that love never dies. That you come to know the energy of a certain loved one is never-ending, and remains with you to support your *own* spiritual journey. The person's energy has only changed appearance. As you come to understand *The Soul Program* explained in the following pages, I hope you exit this book with more peace in your heart knowing that everything that occurs in the life of every soul, whether on this plane or the next, happens for a reason, and is there to help that soul complete its own unique program of learning. And, at the heart of that program is *always* the power of love.

I have heard it said somewhere that death is only the moment when dying ends. I not only know this to be true, I have come to understand it. Dying on this level only means we have completed what we came here to do in *this* body; this form; this time. The Soul has no beginning, and no ending. It just has cumulative experiences. It is in an ongoing journey of evolution. The Soul acts as your awe-inspiring consciousness, your spiritual body, your invisible essence—that eternal part of you that longs to project love, wisdom, caring, compassion, peace, and healing.

We all have a Soul Program and the DPs are there to help us move along with that program. Love survives death. Love lives on—especially deep love. It is in that atmosphere of love that the DPs want to connect and support us. Death is only a part of the cosmic drama. Isn't it time that you become acquainted with what your Soul Program might begin to teach you as the ultimate connector between your human self and the Universe?

Many blessings,

Suzane

acknowledgments

I respectfully thank all who have given me the privilege and honor to connect with loved ones who have crossed over, and those of you who have so generously shared your personal stories. You are the heroes for waking up each day to face, with strength and courage, your loss. I have nothing but the utmost respect for all of you who journey on.

I would like to thank all of my family and friends, who have always been there to support me. To name a few: Sheri Cohen, Libby Jordan, Richard Hein, Faith Busby, Terry and James Platz, Thomas Braccaneri, Ray Preisler, Cindy Northrop, Dennis McMahon, Eileen Kreiger, Denise Goldberg, Eleanor Honig-Skoller, Bobby Four, Tony Fusco, Dennis Assinos, Toni Moore, Billy Degan, and John Holland.

I have had the honor to work and be supported by some of the best in radio and TV: Gary Craig, WTIC, was there from the beginning, and Bob Wolf, WPIX, who went out on a limb during 9/11 in support of my work. Also, Steven Harper, Matty Seigel, and Robin King. I would also like to recognize the many wonderful people I met in all the cities during my travels, who were more than gracious in acknowledging my work.

There are those who are put on earth with a mission to go a step beyond, if not more, to make a difference— those people who go out on a limb in an effort to affect some positive change or growth in the world. That certain group of people, who walk a courageous path that generally risks their reputations, invites ridicule, and provokes comments that they are "nuts." I personally thank those who I have had the honor to work with: Dr. Gary Schwartz for taking a big leap in creating substantial documentation proving the "DPs" do talk; Linda Russet for following in her father's shoes with the desire to find the truth to the question is there life after death, or do we just die; Dr. Mimi Guarneri, who steps beyond the physical care for people's hearts to know someone can die from a broken heart, and that healing a "broken heart" is not just about healing the body but healing the mind and soul as well; and Dr. Bridget Duffy, who is always thinking of ways to share with the world the importance of connecting with loved ones who have crossed over.

I thank Debbie Luican, my publisher, for her vision and mission of Jodere Group that believes life is about making a difference in the world, and for knowing everything happens for a reason. I want to thank all of those who work at Jodere Group for always being more than warm and supportive of my work.

A special thank you goes to Deb Ingersoll of Jodere Group for all the many hours spent orchestrating the book tour, and for always "being there" for me.

A special thanks to Mark Misiano, V.P. and CFO of Jodere Group, for all he does.

To Chad Edwards, my editor—there are no words to express how working with you is not work at all, but rather a dance of passion that always helps me continue to speak my voice and words.

Linda Manning for whom I am constantly in amazement of how she truly cares for every client she talks with. She's a Godsend . . . and my right and left arm.

A thanks goes out to Melanie Burns, who cared and supported me on tour. I thank you from the bottom of my heart.

For Aileen, I couldn't imagine life without you. You are the light at the end of my every tunnel.

And always, my humble thanks and gratitude to the DPs, who have taught me over and over again a great lesson . . . life and love are eternal.

introduction

For 25 years, I've been working as a trance medium, and I've come to enjoy an international reputation for integrity, accuracy, and responsibility. Beginning with my first experience visiting with Dead People, at age 13, when my grandmother, who had just died, came to see me; I often wondered why others had such difficulty with something that seemed so natural that I didn't even think to question it.

In the years that followed, I found myself orchestrating a life with people along the way who encouraged me and who would continuously urge me to accept and appreciate the powerful gift I've been blessed with. As time went by, with their help and my own growing sense of comfort with my "calling," I came to understand that my ability to converse with

Dead People was more than just what some defined as an *abnormality*.

I began to see that I had an obligation to use that ability to help other people communicate with their loved ones because that's what talking to the dead is all about—LOVE. Not only our love for those who've passed over, but also their love for us. Not only about our need to communicate messages of love to "them," but their desire to communicate their messages of love and life to us. I've come to understand that's why all those DPs have been so anxious to make themselves known to me. It wasn't because they enjoyed my company or because they were trying to make me nuts; it was because they knew I was a receptive conduit, and that I had the ability to convey their messages to loved ones on this plane. Everything happens for a reason.

What I've discovered over those years is that the Dead People need to let us know that they're alright. They want us to understand that if they were in pain, the pain is gone; if they were sick, they're now healed; if there was a rift between them and us, as far as they're concerned, it's been mended. It's their job to tell us these things so we might become free, and it's our job to listen—*learn* to listen in a broader sense. It is from the deep love they have for us that they wish us to learn how to let go, and to move on as best we can toward fulfilling the lessons of our *own* Soul Program.

As you bravely continue to examine the relationship between those who have passed over, your own soul, and your own Soul Program, I believe you will come to realize you actually live a dual existence. There are two selves at play here. There is the self of the personality and all its earthly expressions, but we are much more than our personality, and there is the self that is the higher, endless, invisible, immeasurable self—your *Soul Self*. The personality acts as a mask. It is important for you to learn that the personality of the human self is the actor upon the stage of the human drama. It is the personality's program to create the experiences for our souls so we may have the opportunity to learn the lessons designated by our soul's program. We choose the personalities that are going to best serve whatever is in accordance with each individual's Soul Program. The people we choose as our parents, and their personalities, also influence our personalities. And, all the individual personality learns in one lifetime will go into a *Soul Bank*. As we choose to reincarnate, we can draw upon that bank of learning to support the lifetime we are entering. The Earth's program is difficult. That is why we learn so much. Sometimes the learning comes from the experience created by the personality, and not the person. Once we are born, the personality is born, and that's it for that particular lifetime. And, as you will have free will as the personality, the soul's choices have been set by the soul's program for that lifetime. This also explains how in one family of many children that they can be so different.

The Soul Self, or individual soul, is like a planet in the total universe of cosmic life that we call the Soul of God, the Oversoul. With The Soul Program, we have the opportunity of growing and expanding our energy and consciousness to become more and more like the Oversoul, or God consciousness. This is what we refer to as the evolution of the Soul. It doesn't matter if you are skeptical in regards to what you are about to read. I love a healthy skeptic. What I do know is that if you surrender to examining the things that happen in your life and why they might happen, you will begin to see, hear, touch, and experience life from an entirely different perspective. And you might just come to know yourself as you really are.

I can't personally explain, scientifically, *how* this communication occurs. But I do, absolutely, know why. The why—and I'll probably be saying this over and over in the course of this book—is the continuing power and energy of love. The continuum of love— ours for those who've passed over and theirs for us—is at the core of what I do, and what I have come to define as *The Soul Program*. Scientists will continue to discuss and investigate and write about their findings, but I *know* those people who've passed over aren't "dead" in the way we've come to think of that word. Sure, they're not having dinner with us every night, they're not coming home from work or school each day, they're not physically inhabiting our lives, but they *do* know what's going on with us, and we *can* know what's going on with them.

chapter one

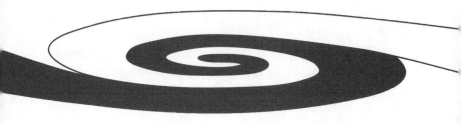

making contact

*Every relationship that touches the soul
leads us into a dialogue with eternity, so that,
even though we may think our strong emotions focus on
the people around us, we are being set face to face with
divinity itself, however we understand or speak that mystery.*

— THOMAS MOORE

a lthough by now talking to Dead Folks is, for me,
a totally natural experience, I realize that for
many of you this may be your first adventure into
this work, or there might still be questions for those
of you who are continuing to learn about it. In an
effort to lead you toward a clearer understanding of
why things occur, I'd like to start off by doing a
quick review of exactly what it is that takes place
when I am preparing myself to make contact, so you
may start to understand this communication coming
from a higher realm.

My intention here is, that along the way, I answer some questions you might have about making contact, why contacts are made, why things happen, and what resolves are possible and what lessons can be learned through some of the contacts as I have experienced them. I will try to help you understand why the contacts are made in the way they are, and give some examples of the messages given by those loved ones who have crossed over. I do this also because I want to help you realize that because you are bound to those loved ones in some way who have passed over—and they to you—that you, too, have the power to communicate.

Most of us, 99 percent I would guess, have already had communication with the other side as children. You know, those imaginary friends that we were eventually told to abandon because, "You are too old to be doing that now. What will people think?" They never left us. We were taught to move away from them. Therefore, this book is in part about helping you to understand on a greater level, and for some, maybe for the first time, that you can reconnect to that part of you that was inherent and natural from the beginning to get some answers to the questions you have been living with.

Throughout this reading, I would like for you to carry with you the reality that we only experience limitation in the body, sometimes in the mind, but when it comes to Spirit, in all its magnificence, there is no limitation. There is nothing that Spirit, the Soul Consciousness, cannot accomplish through love. I am sure we have all had an experience where we did not know how something was going to happen, yet, because we believed without reservation from the very core of our being that somehow it would happen, it did. We have all had those moments when the "light of understanding" goes on where previously we have been in darkness. That, for me, is the beauty and the power of the journey of the soul. Truly, nothing is impossible! It is all in how you choose to look at things. How and what you believe. I have always thought that Albert Einstein said it best: *There are only two ways to live your life. One is as though nothing is a miracle. The other is as though everything is a miracle.*

Let's start by looking at some others' thoughts about "why everything happens for a reason" taken from the message board on my Website.

FIRST SHARE

I can only relate to you what has happened time and time again in my own life. Everytime something has happened to me on my own life journey, it has become clear to me further on why things happened the way they did; choices I've made, things that have happened that were out of my control, everything happens for a reason. I lost my mom when I was 25 years old (and seven months pregnant). I was so angry and filled with grief, I pushed away other people in my life who needed me. I almost lost everything else that was important to me. Coming to terms with the "why" of major life events is probably the biggest opportunity for growth you can have. I can tell you that with time everything becomes clear and you should try to focus on the positive things that will happen as a result of major events in your life.

SECOND SHARE

I do believe that everything happens for a reason, but not necessarily your reason. By that, I mean that very life-shaking events can happen to you, but not so much for your own development as for the development of someone else you are connected to. If someone you love dies, it could be more important for them to move to their next level and not necessarily that you have some valuable lesson to learn simply by hurting. I don't think God wants us to hurt like that. But I think it is necessary to be temporarily separated from those we have grown to love just so that they can continue on their path. But we meet them again.

THIRD SHARE

Boy, do I hear you when you talk about the pursuit of the big "why." How much time I have spent trying to understand some things, events, life shifts, and experiences. Of course, the losses have great impact. Someone once taught me to follow every "Why?" with a "Why not?" and see where it takes me. That has worked sometimes, sometimes not. My spiritual mentor also taught me to go quickly to look for the "gift" in every situation. That has helped over time immensely. Time can help, I believe, by providing some distance from the loss. How one heals depends on what they do with that time. I eventually do come to a point, though, that I do have some understanding of what has happened and for what reason. Thanks for the feedback. This one is something that I continually explore.

FOURTH SHARE

You're on the right path. How you deal with life's twists and turns will make all the difference. If you train yourself to always look for one positive thing about every situation, you won't get bogged down in would have, could have, should have, you know, the famous, "what if . . . ?" One positive thought will lead to more.

FIFTH SHARE

I have come to the realization that the "why" things happen is not nearly important for people as the "why didn't this happen." For instance, "Why couldn't we just stay in love?" or "Why couldn't they save my sister in the accident?" There is no truer saying then the one that tells us that we learn nothing from a lifetime filled with happiness. Think of all the most difficult heartbreaking experiences and how much you have learned from them. It may seem like needless suffering and that the world distributes its share of happiness unfairly, but that is simply not true. For instance, I have a sister who has everything: career, family, job, money. Others may see that she has all of this, but how many know that she lost her only son two years prior. Through grief and devastation we all became closer, of course you are never the same really, but it made me start to really live, not to worry about the little things that I never really found important. You have a blueprint for yourself, as simplistic as it may seem, you chose your path before your soul came here. People make too much out of life. It is short, but I would rather take difficult situations in stride and take time to enjoy what I have already. Stop asking "why" and start asking, "what now" in a positive way!

You see, this question—why do things happen for a reason—comes to everyone's mind at one time or another. With that, let me share with you just how the connection to the other side happens so we can begin our voyage toward understanding the soul and why I believe all things happen for a reason.

connection and delivery

Because I'm going to be using my mind to "tune-in," quite literally, to a frequency that is quite different from the one we use for everyday verbal communication, it's necessary for me to begin to "tune-out" of that earthbound frequency several hours in advance.

Our brain has two hemispheres, each of which governs specific modes of thinking. The left side of the brain is logical, rational, and analytical, while the right side is intuitive, random, and holistic. Usually with any individual, one side is more fully developed than the other. That's why some people are great at math and science (left brain) while others are more creative and "artistic" (right brain). Since I started out to be a composer and have been trained as a musician, and let me say here that there is a great deal of mathematics in creating music, I've probably always been more geared to right-brain than left-brain orientation. Therefore, when I know I'm going to be communicating with the DPs, I begin to consciously turn down the volume on my logical, or left brain, and turn up my intuitive, or right brain, at least three hours before the work is to begin, so that upon arrival at a retreat situation, séance, or any group sitting, I have been in an altered state for hours already. The same process happens when I do lectures or seminars. I have to be more aware of the delivery in the respect that I have to also make this interesting and provide factual explanations about *what* I do and *how* I do it. That is definitely part of what the people seem to want when they attend. After all, this is my work, and with any "job" there comes certain responsibilities. And those responsibilities are running two-fold during any session where I am connecting. The DPs have their responsibilities also. I will explain this in more detail when we get to the chapter on The Boundary Program.

Most of the time the DPs start talking before I even arrive at an event, but it is no longer a problem. (There is a familiar pattern I sense at their arrival. We have also made an "agreement" as to when I am ready to "receive.") By the time I enter a room, I am already in an altered state of receiving. I may appear cognizant of what I am doing, but since I am not in a left-brain consciousness, it becomes automatic what I receive and convey at that point. I must prepare myself to be in the moment so that I can be open to whatever might come through. This is where my music background and improvisation with music has supported me. To do this, one has to be comfortable with a large element of spontaneity. I have to come from a place of giving myself over in trust. I have to totally give myself over to Spirit. Nothing planned. No probing questions beforehand of the attendees. This explains why I talk fast, and sometimes use humor or wit to balance out the energy, so that a loving element comes through about the message. It is not my intention or the DPs' to come across harsh and cruel. Remember this is about love.

Psychologists or psychiatrists might talk about what I do in Freudian terms as engaging in a kind of self-hypnosis, which involves quieting the ego or conscious, pragmatic, logical part of the mind in order to allow the subconscious to roam free. You might understand what I mean here a bit better if you think about it like this: think of a time when you were doing something where you were so engrossed in *what* you were doing that you completely lost track of time. Now, you were still present on some level, yet totally engaged in the moment. Some master teachers would say you are immersed in your *bliss*—that place where you are completely open to all the Universe has to offer. It is magic what happens in that space and with that kind of connection. This is the way it is with me. I am totally enveloped in the frequencies, or vibrations, at this time of the DPs, and they with me, so that we can communicate and deliver the messages. (I will talk more about the vibrational synchronicities later on.) You can think about it in whatever terms make you most comfortable, but I prefer to talk about tuning-in and changing frequencies because what I do is, in fact, all about entering or aligning my mind with vibrations from another plane, almost as if I were some kind of psychic radio transmitter and receiver.

Energy creates vibrations (and remember that energy never dies), but different energy levels create different vibrations. While we're on this plane, we're in our physical bodies, which are dense and, therefore, lower the vibrations that emanate from our energy. When we pass over and shed our physical bodies, those vibrations rise to a faster, higher frequency, which is why most people aren't able (or think they aren't able) to tune into them. In fact, fine-tuning your radio would be a perfect analogy. If you're not quite on the right frequency, you'll get a lot of static and it will be harder to hear what the broadcast is sending out; but once you've hit the station exactly, the words or music will be louder and clearer.

In order to make contact with the DPs, I have to raise the frequency of my vibrations, and they—because they want to communicate—have to lower theirs, until we are, effectively, both tuned-in to the same frequency. I am, in effect, acting as the radio receiver, receiving signals and broadcasting them to my clients. That's why, while I'm in this altered state, I speak much more quickly and my voice is pitched higher than when I'm talking normally. Not to mention that it is like an opera and all the cast is trying to come through at one time to deliver their performance (message).

The fact that the DPs no longer have a physical body accounts not only for their change in "frequency," but also for the fact that they so often communicate electronically—by causing the lights, the radio, or the television to go on and off, for example. Without a physical body, they are nothing more than disembodied, vibratory energy. Sending electronic signals to notify us of their presence is one of the most effective ways they have of communicating. These sorts of phenomena occur most frequently shortly after someone has passed, usually during the first year, but also on special dates such as holidays or the anniversary of their death. If something like this happens to you, don't let it "freak you out," and don't be too quick to call the electrician. It might just be your loved one coming to call!

Here are a couple of examples:

One client of mine told me a particularly touching and remarkable story about this kind of "electronic" communication. She had lost one of her twin daughters and, every night since her daughter's death, the light in the surviving twin's room had gone on and off of it's own accord. Both mother and daughter were so used to this phenomenon and so comforted by the nightly communication that, after a while, it simply became a part of their everyday lives. After the tragedy at the World Trade Center, however, my client was so upset, that she went into her daughter's room and asked the twin in spirit to "please, go help those people." From that day on, the light stopped going on and off until, several months later, my client began to miss her dead daughter's communications and asked her to come back. Shortly after she made that loving request, the light began to go on and off again.

Another client explained that when her husband, and father of the household, had passed, the family wanted to include with him articles that were significant to his personality. Besides adding tennis shoes and sweat bottoms to his suit jacket and tie, they all knew he would be lost without his remote control. With that, they just grabbed the remote that was always either in his hand or at his lounger side. Everyone at the funeral had remarked that seeing Ed holding his remote was certainly amusing and indicative of his personality. That evening as extended family and friends left the house gathering following the funeral, the wife and children sat down to just "numb out" in front of the TV. They were exhausted and had run out of words at that point. You know, the silence that is left when you are first left alone after a loss. They had to turn on the TV "by hand" and were sitting not speaking to each other. They all had blank stares as they looked toward the screen. Suddenly, the TV went off. They turned it back on. Off it went again, and again they turned it back on. It went off a third time. They all looked at each other in disbelief, then a burst of laughter exploded in the room. Surely, they knew that Ed was letting them know he was still around, and still had control.

communication and the communicators

I always keep the lights dimmed so that no one in the room will have to feel like they're in the spotlight or that other people are staring at them, especially at séances. I also try to do this, as best as possible, at lectures and seminars. Some of the information coming forth can be quite personal, although it is not usually the purpose of the DP to cause embarrassment. A little fun, maybe. I always begin by reciting a prayer. For me, saying a prayer is a way to acknowledge the Higher Power that I know exists, and to say thank you, both for the powers that have been given and for the free will to use them.

By this time, the DPs are usually clamoring to come through, and sometimes the cacophony of their various messages can feel like a psychic bombardment from above. Think of it this way, in a séance of six to twelve people—the usual number—each person may have two or more relatives or loved ones trying to come through. Another way to think of this is that you have ten to twelve children all trying to get your attention at the same time. We've all been there.

This is always true with my seminars and lectures with the numbers involved. But it became particularly overwhelming after the events of September 11 in New York City. As you may know, I live there and was home at the time. I just remember feeling as though these phenomenal electrical jolts were going through my body right after the World Trade Center (WTC) Towers came down. Needless to say, the bombardment immediately afterwards of those who had passed over wanting to let those left behind know right away they were okay was overwhelming.

One woman who attended a séance at about the time of the WTC disaster heard not only from the person she'd lost but also from two other people whose names she didn't even know. Only later, when she inquired as to who these two unknown fellows might be, did she find out they'd been two of her friend's best buddies, who'd also been lost that day. And that, by the way, is just about the most irrefutable sort of validation any medium could receive. If the woman herself was unaware of these people's existence, where could I have been getting the information except from the DPs themselves?

But, however many souls there are trying to get a word in edgewise, it's usually the ones with the strongest, most determined personalities (and they're usually the ones who were that way in life) whose messages come through first. The quiet, shrinking violets just have to wait their turn—but they will get their turn. It's not in my control, but the DPs seem to have arranged it so that no one gets shut out.

Communicating with the DPs is not like holding a normal conversation. I can't just ask them questions and get back answers in complete, cohesive sentences. Sometimes I just receive a word or even a strong physical sensation. I also want to say here that we never see DPs directly—always peripherally. That is not to say that people do not see DPs, it is just that to appear is the least form of connection. The number one way the DPs communicate is through dreams because the right brain is more in the foreground when you are more relaxed and there is no interference. Another reason for this is because in the dreamstate, you are not startled by the fact that they appear as you would be if they just "showed up" when you were awake. Other favorite ways to communicate are through music, children, animals, and smells. They will mostly make contact with someone when they are engaged in nonlinear activities—when the left brain is at the "rear." They love the car and radios.

There are many people that have had all types of communications through some form of numbers. As we all know, numbers were significant throughout the Bible. Then there are other things. Recently a friend, whose father had been verbally abusive to his wife and children, underwent surgery for throat cancer. His surgery took place on the very day that his wife died of cancer 20 years earlier.

Next is a note from the message board on my Website that also talks about connection through numbers.

> I attended Suzane's seminar in Seattle on June 24, 2002. The Thursday prior to the seminar (on Monday night), I was fortunate to connect and talk with Suzane during one of her radio interviews.
>
> I was on hold for approximately 25–26 minutes. When she came on the phone and asked who I wanted to connect to, the time was 8:36 A.M. or 24 minutes to 9 o'clock.
>
> I said I wanted to connect to my son. Then, afterwards, I began to look at the numbers.
>
> Here's the information compared to the times:
>
> ➢ My son was born 9/24/68 and died 3/14/93.
>
> ➢ The numbers were all there except the number 14. Then, I showed this to my brother like this: 8:36, 24-9.
>
> ➢ He then said this: add 8 and 36 together = 44
>
> ➢ Subtract 9 from 24 = 15
>
> ➢ Add 44 + 15 = 59
> 5 + 9 = 14
>
> The way that it was put on paper there wasn't very much manipulation of the numbers to come up with this.

Then, just last week, I was watching John Edward with my wife and mentioned that I wish I would have asked Suzane the common number between my son and I when I talked to her on the phone.

My wife responded to me when I asked her if she remembered and she said "Yes, it was 29."

She reminded me that it was our favorite number on the roulette wheel and that the last time we were together was in Reno, Nevada before his death.

Not more than 15 seconds had past when some commercial I had never seen on TV was advertising a special price for the product it was selling. The cost appeared in big numbers on the screen: $29.95. Here was the numbers 29 and 14 at the same time.

I believe my son was right there and listening to the conversation.

Probably, because of my musical background, the messages I receive are primarily auditory or phonetic. I'll hear the sound of a name or a relationship or some other identifying characteristic. Sometimes all I get is an "e" or an "i" or an "f" sound, or some other phonetic signal. The "i" sound might mean Ivan, but it might also mean Eileen. Very often names act like keys for me in that they provide the entry into the connection. Once that is given and someone validates the name, it is like the door is swinging open and the rest of the information comes through. I have no idea what they mean, so as I receive them and convey them to the sitters in the room, it's up to each person there to make the connection to someone in spirit who is meaningful to him or her. They will usually follow with something else to support the name that is trying to come through: a situation, an article—like something passed down through the family—something unique that a family member or loved one would recognize. It is also quite common that they could bring along a pet. That's where the personal dynamics among the people in the room come in as well. I find, often, that people with loved ones having the same name, type of death, or gender will effect how people are clustered in the room to receive messages.

The DPs usually give me a general sense of where the person they're connected to is sitting, so I'm able to point myself in the approximate direction of the person I *think* I'm supposed to be speaking to, but the attendees often have their own ideas about that. Just as there are those in spirit who are more forthcoming or aggressive than others, there are usually those among the living who are more eager to "claim" a message than some of the others. Sometimes there's one person who thinks that every message—no matter whom *I* might think it's directed toward—is meant for him or her. Other, more timid members of the group might also think they understand the message but decline to speak up and claim it. I can try to indicate that the DP is telling me it's on my left, but if the "claimee" on my right continues to be insistent, there's really nothing I can do about it. I just have to let the living sort it out for themselves.

In fact, the dead often seem to be much more disciplined than the living. After that first noisy clamoring for attention, they almost seem to line up and wait their turn, so that I'm able to go around the room and deliver their messages with some semblance of order. Some DP, who's particularly anxious, might interrupt from time to time, and if there's an animal present he might be yipping around everyone's heels, but usually, once they've sorted themselves out, they are a pretty polite bunch.

It does happen on occasion that a DP will *think* he or she is giving the most significant identifying information, but the person he's trying to reach simply isn't "getting it." More often than not, when that happens, it's because the one who's living just isn't thinking fast enough. Or sometimes, thinking too hard. At one recent séance, there were seven women in the room. One of the DPs kept showing me a crystal and telling me it was highly significant to his loved one. As it can be sometimes, practically everyone was claiming a connection to the crystal. There wasn't anyone who didn't have some of her mother's or grandmother's or aunt's crystals, but no one seemed to think it was very significant—until finally, one shrinking violet, who'd been totally silent on the subject up to that moment, timidly suggested that she had a large collection of quartz crystals and that some of them were actually of museum quality. At that point, her loved one told me to tell her that she'd been "much smarter" when he was alive!

When a DP keeps insisting that his or her message is significant, and the one for whom it's meant either can't or won't claim it, there's sometimes nothing I can do but "leave it" with the person for whom I believe it's intended, and trust that he or she will sort it out eventually. Sometimes, however, another DP connected to that person will step in and offer further validating data to clear up the confusion. The name Fred, for example, might not be immediately significant, but if someone else comes forward and says his name is Eric and he's Fred's brother or son or grandfather, putting the two names together might just provide the jolt that's needed to register the connection. As I've said, the dead often seem to be a lot smarter than the living.

I remember one evening, recently, while I was on tour that will illustrate my point about speaking up.

It had been a really wonderful evening at this particular seminar and I was nearing the close when something sent me straight to the back of the room toward two young men sitting next to each other. I was sure I had some messages for them. I kept giving the information that the DP was giving me and the two kept looking at me like I had completely lost it. Both looked at each other and said they didn't have a clue what I was talking about. Every time I started to leave to return to the platform, the DP would not let me go telling me that I had to get this message across and to go back until it was delivered and understood. I went back and told the two men that

I knew this was for them. I gave the name, told about the man's belt buckle being passed down to a boy, and that their had been two children that had drowned that were with him there now. It was really becoming humorous for the two young men, the rest of the room and myself. I finally said I was just going to deliver the information and started to turn to leave them when a woman seated next to the two young men spoke up and said, "That was for me. That was my husband." I stopped, turned, and must have looked like someone had slapped me because the whole room broke into laughter. Here I had been talking to the two men for about 15 minutes, refusing to go, and the person the message was for was sitting right next to them saying not a word. Because I was so intent on delivering the messages to them, she didn't speak up. She was not with them and didn't know them.

Therefore, if you think the message coming through is for you, speak up.

In addition to the auditory messages I receive, I also "feel" physical sensations, which are often related to the DP's cause of death. For example, I might feel a heaviness in my chest if someone passed as the result of a heart attack or my breathing might be restricted if the cause of death was lung disease. These sensations are not prolonged; they come and go very quickly, and sometimes I might not be able to tell if someone actually died of lung disease or if they were just a heavy smoker. I might also, at times, have some difficulty determining if a sensation in the chest is related to the heart or the lungs—although these are usually different feelings. But, once again, it's up to the living to pick up on and validate what I'm feeling.

I also "see" in my mind's eye, so to speak, visual images, such as a man in uniform or a small child in a red dress, or a young woman with blonde hair. Very often, the image of a particular pet lying or running around close to one of the DPs is just the validating piece of information someone in the room needs to assure them that this DP "belongs" to them. But none of these images is anything like what one thinks of as ghosts who materialize the way George and Marian Kirby did in the *Cosmo Topper* movies and TV series.

Ghosts are, in fact, the souls of dead folk who either have chosen not to leave the place they were on earth or who, usually after a sudden or violent death, don't yet accept the fact that they're dead and no longer have a physical body. These souls possibly didn't either believe in life after death, or the trauma of their death left them somewhat disoriented and not realizing they are indeed, dead. The soul is not making the conscious connection of the fact that they have left the physical body.

An example of this would be the many stories of all the young men that were killed in the American Civil War. Throughout the southern states there have been sightings for years in wooded areas, southern homes, and barns. It would appear that these young men chose many of these places to hide out from the enemy and then were killed. There are also stories of them roaming the battlefields. They are in a sense "trapped." In the first instance, the ghost is in the place he chose to be—of his own free will—and where he will stay until he chooses to move on. The spirit might be like the character (in both senses of the word) in the movie *Ghost*, who chooses, for whatever reason, to remain in the subway, where he died. Maybe just so he can terrorize poor unsuspecting spirits like Sam, the young boyfriend who's murdered at the beginning of the movie, as his kind of revenge against those who murdered him before, what he considered, "his time."

In the second instance (a sudden or violent death), the soul is literally trapped between two worlds, like Sam, and must remain close to the place where he or she died, or close to a living loved one until someone on this plane—be it an exorcist, a shaman, a priest, or a medium that does what is called "rescue work"—is able to make contact and convince the ghost-soul to let go of his or her connection to this plane and move on. But, as I said, it's not ghosts that I "see" in these sessions. And, these DPs have a hard time communicating with us.

While we're on the subject, however, I might as well add that there were many things that *Ghost* portrayed quite accurately, such as the fact that Sam didn't immediately seem to realize he had passed, and that he appeared to be "hanging around" to make sure the woman he was in love with was protected from danger. One scene, whose accuracy actually made me laugh, is the one in which poor Whoopi Goldberg, as Oda Mae, is being bombarded by voices from the spirit world trying to make themselves heard. As I've said, that's often the way it appears to me at the beginning, when so many DPs are gathered and clamoring to deliver their messages.

Of course, there were other instances where the movie took generous cinematic license, such as Sam and Oda Mae's having normal, completely rational conversations, or Sam's being able to wrestle with Carl. Those in spirit can move objects with the power of their energy, but actually pushing around or engaging in physical combat with the living is simply not, as a rule, something they do. I have had an occasion where people have told me they have had a physical contact. Some have felt their loved ones sit on the bed with them, or felt a brush on the cheek. I'm one who does not wish to negate people's experiences. Who am I to say what has or has not happened to a person? It's their experience. At any rate, most connection is not in a dramatic sense. It's not like Hollywood. It's not like the *Sixth Sense,* although Bruce Willis's character was in the same position as was Sam in that he also didn't realize he had passed. Most connections are usually very subtle and come through in a way only you are going to know.

So let's continue the explanation of how messages are sent. The DPs use many methods—auditory, physical, visual, and also olfactory. I often experience a variety of smells or aromas, such as tobacco smoke, perfumes, fragrances, or flowers, and very often other people in the room are able to smell them as well, particularly if several of the DPs were smokers. And sometimes it's just the aroma of a particular perfume wafting through the room that let's a person know his loved one is present. These are the most common. As I've learned over time, the DPs can be extremely creative when they want to make their presence known.

A good example of this was when I was appearing on a well-known TV show in the northwest United States. A woman that I ended up delivering messages to, from her father, said that the day before she had come to the show she continually smelled the tobacco aroma of her father's cigars. Her house was a non-smoking house. So, sometimes the loved one will give us a signal that they are around or about to make their presence known in a stronger way.

disconnecting

No matter what the venue, be it séance, lecture, or seminar, it always follows a natural progression, from the opening clamor to the more organized chaos to the ultimate fading of energy from the other side, and it generally lasts from 2 to 2½ hours. By that time I'm completely exhausted—this is extremely rewarding but also tremendously demanding work—and the room is always filled with emotions that can run the gamut from intense feelings of love to equally intense hostility.

Although the DPs are always there to express their love, those in the room may still be harboring anger at the departed for something that occurred before he or she passed, or guilt about something they believe they did wrong or maybe failed to do. That's one of the main reasons people sometimes fail or refuse to acknowledge the message one of the DPs may be trying to deliver. The living sometimes just can't understand that the dead have moved on, not only from this plane, but also from whatever "issues" may have been plaguing their relationships with their loved ones on earth. If there are negative emotions in the room, they always come from the living, *never* from the dead. And, as the term "medium" implies, I am the conduit for all the positive and negative vibrations emanating from both sides. Sometimes this "tossing" back and forth of emotional vibrations is like being on *spin dry*.

It's probably exhausting for the DPs, too, because I'm not the only one using my energies to make the level of my vibrations compatible with theirs. They're also adjusting their frequencies to tune into mine. By the end of the allotted time, I can feel their vibrations receding, and then I know that it's time to close the door. At that point, I always thank the dead folks for coming, and I slowly begin to separate from the spirit world, gradually returning to my normal state of consciousness, a process that can take several hours after the session to complete.

It's invariably an intensely emotional and exhilarating experience for everyone in the room. Quite often many tears have been shed, whether of joy, relief, or sorrow, almost always, many laughs have been shared, and there are generally a few surprises as well. The DPs don't lose their sense of humor when they pass, and often it's the reminder of an amusing characteristic—Uncle Herman always was the loudest most boisterous member of the family, so of course he'd be the first one to come through—or a happy relationship—Little Nipper always did love to stand on his hind legs and lick mama's face—that provides just the validation that someone in the room is looking for.

Very often, when someone knows they are coming for an event in which I will be giving readings or a séance, they'll ask silently, aloud, or in whatever way their comfortable, that the people they most wish to hear from will come through. But that doesn't always mean that it will happen, nor does it mean that there won't be others who make their presence known as well. I always tell people before every session that whatever their expectations are, they should set them aside because the experience probably won't be what they imagined, it isn't logical, and they may be hearing from folks they haven't even thought about in years.

Because I've effectively shut down my left, logical, analytical brain for the duration, I rarely remember anything that's happened during the session, unless someone chooses to share his or her experiences with me afterwards. I can feel the emotions that are left in the room, but I can't necessarily identify their source. And that's fine with me. I know I'm not meant to remember and, in any case, it would be impossibly draining to retain all the feelings that pass through me from one plane to the other.

No matter what has transpired, however, and despite my exhaustion, I'm always left with a sense of gratitude for the gift and the privilege I've been given to help people. Being able to answer some of the questions that may have been haunting their lives, or preventing them from arriving at a resolution with the past, and moving on with the learning they have yet to do, is always rewarding.

how messages are delivered

One of the questions I'm asked most frequently, by those who are trying to communicate with a loved one who has passed, is whether they can be sure the person they're trying to contact will "come through" for them. Sometimes, yes. Sometimes, no. Often their concerns are practical in nature: "My little girl was only a year old, she wasn't even talking, how will she be able to communicate with me?" Or "Great Aunt Tillie only spoke Russian and you only speak English, so how will you know what she's trying to say?"

In these instances, I can assure the questioners that what they perceive as barriers won't prevent their making contact. If a child is too young to speak, he or she will either have grown up in spirit or there will be an older family member with him or her to provide validating information so that the parent will be certain to recognize the child. And, for reasons I truly can't explain, when *Aunt Tillie* needs or wants to communicate through me, she will miraculously become fluent in English, although she will have a recognizably Russian accent. I can only assume that somewhere "out there" there's a multilingual psychic translator doing a really good job.

Aside from these practical assurances, however, I can't ever guarantee who will come through in any given situation. That decision is really up to the DPs themselves. Most people think that because this is what I do—my gift—that I can call on a certain DP at will—anytime I wish—and they will come. For my part, the answer is, not always. I do know, however, that any message that is supposed to get through *will* get through. Sometimes the problem lies with those who are still among the living, and who have very specific preconceived notions of who they expect to make contact, what they want to hear, and who is to deliver the message.

A vivid example of just that sort of thing occurred while I was on a radio call-in program:

> A gentleman caller asked me to contact his father, who had passed recently, but he simply wasn't coming through strongly for me. Instead, there was another man, who seemed, as it turned out, to be the caller's grandfather,

insistent on making his presence known. And, he seemed to be holding a fishing rod. When I conveyed this information to the man on the phone, there was a long silence, after which he said, "That's my father's father. He was a fisherman. I don't want to speak with him. I want to hear from my father." I could detect some angst in the voice of the caller. Although it was difficult (to say the least) to convince the caller that it was his grand-father's message that was supposed to come through at this time, and that the grand-father was trying to heal the rift in their rela-tionship, and tell his grandson that he loved him. He also said he wanted to say he was sorry for all the pain his passing had caused. The caller, however, simply didn't want to hear that message, and wanted only to hear from his father. That's the problem with some of us on this plane—we can be awfully stubborn.

I was getting a sharp pain in my head and told this gentleman that I could assure him that *his* father was present with his father, and yet, *his* father was standing aside to let the grandfather say what he needed to. Quite often when many DPs are present, certain ones will step back because they know a stronger message needs to come through for the healing of someone present. I asked about the grandfather and his passing, and my caller said that the grandfather had shot his wife and then turned the gun on himself dying of a gunshot wound to the head. That explained the pain I was feeling on one side of my head. It appeared that the grandfather had been a notable presence in the community and this had caused the family a great deal of pain and embarrassment. It was something that all the family had carried for years—tucked away and never emotionally addressed. There had been no understanding or answers as to the "why." The caller had been his grandfather's favorite grandchild and spent many hours with him fishing. He had been only 12 and visiting his grandparents on the weekend of the tragic incident. This man I was talking to had never been able to move on from that horrific happening. He had felt abandoned, and also carried some guilt that he hadn't been able to do something to prevent it, just as he had felt recently with his own father's death of alcoholism.

As I closed with the caller there seemed to be some understanding. I can only hope so. I've never had any follow-up with the man. We all feel that abandoned, to some degree, when a parent passes over. It's like suddenly you feel orphaned. You question in some cases what you might have done to prevent the passing, or were you a good son or daughter. And, no matter what age we are when we lose a parent, suddenly there is no longer that safety net to "lean on." This is especially true for young children experiencing a parent or close friend's death. Even though the man's father was present, and he desperately wanted to connect with him, as in this case, it may simply be that a particular DP will step back and let what *they* feel is the stronger message to come through. Remember they are making contact to promote healing so one can move on in their life. It doesn't mean that contact won't be made at another time with the loved one you are seeking.

There is another reason that sometimes you may not make contact with the person you want to and that is simply that they, the DP, may at that moment, be too distant to pick up the information. In such a case, that person just wasn't meant to come through at that particular moment. Or, there may be other impediments to the communication. A person might be harboring negative emotions, such as resentment or jealousy that would hinder the contact. Or one of the dead folk might realize that a particular person is not yet psychologically prepared to receive his message. In the case above, the grandfather quite possibly felt it was time to contact his grandson, probably because of the recent death of the father. Something signaled it was time to deal with other past issues that might have cause to impede this man's progress in moving on through his own father's passing toward resolve and closure. The DPs clearly want us to heal our wounds so we can move forward on our own soul's journey.

Sometimes a DP knows that his or her loved one is not the best person to receive his message, and he'll pick someone else—someone he knows will be willing to listen—to deliver the message for him. The following letter explains how just this sort of thing happened to a client of mine who had been desperately trying to find a way to contact her 17-year-old son, David. I told this story in my last book, *Second Chance*, but it is worth repeating:

> As often as I've practiced the meditation that you walked us through the day of the intimate workshop, I was never really sure if I was "getting anything." As you so often talk about, I kept negating most of what I think I saw or heard. I had this preconceived notion that when I saw something in my mind's eye it wasn't clear enough, or too clear, so none of it could be real. You took us through the meditation and emphasized that we were not to question what we saw, smelled, or heard. I thought, "Here I go again. I'm going to be the only person in the room to either not get anything or not be able to impart what I think I got." I was also thinking that we were wasting all this time and all I wanted to hear was if David was around. But I went through the meditation. Suddenly, the face of a little boy appeared. I knew he was approximately four years old. I also knew more than I saw that he had brown hair and very blue eyes, and that he wanted me to "tell Mommy I love her." As you instructed us, I wrote all this down. One by one, we each recited the information we had "supposedly" received. There was

another woman in the room who said she had a friend who was not present who had lost a son named Kevin. You supportively validated my connection with more information before we ended.

A couple of weeks later I was driving home and, as I often do now since the loss of my son, I turned off the radio and just let my mind clear . . . I was in that state of mind and clearly the name "Katie" and then your name, "Suzane Northrop," came to me. Remembering what you'd said, I just went with it and those two names kept coming to me. I thought, "Hot diggedy dog, Suzane's DPs are coming through me. When I get home, I'm going to just leave a message on her answering machine and see if she has a relative named Katie."

When I arrived home, I only had fifteen minutes before I had to leave for a meeting at Compassionate Friends, a wonderful support group for people who have lost children. So I put off the phone call until later. At the meeting, there was a young woman I'd never seen before talking about how a friend of hers had gone to a psychic a couple of weeks before and, though she knew nothing about psychics, her friend had relayed to her that someone in the room had said they'd seen a little boy about four-years-old named Kevin and to "tell Mommy I love her." The woman said that although she really didn't put much stock in the "psychic stuff," she couldn't help believing that this was her son. Another woman in the room said, "Katie, what's the psychic's name?" Katie replied, "Suzane Northrop."

I just about fell off my chair. I shared with Katie, after the meeting, that I'd been the one who'd had a connection with her son. She had a button on her blouse with a picture of Kevin on it, and I was stunned by how similar he looked to what I'd seen, especially the "very blue eyes." Katie threw her arms around me and through tears thanked me profusely. I was completely overwhelmed that I'd been able to give her a moment with her son again.

I truly trust now the conversations I have in my head with my son and I seldom question the things I experience during meditation, or that happen daily, as they are significant of my son's continued presence and love in my life.

— MOLLIE

Clearly, it was no coincidence that Mollie was at the same workshop as Katie's friend. Coincidence, as I always say, is just our way of explaining the synergies we can't or don't want to attribute to powers we don't understand. And, as this experience so dramatically illustrates, the DPs will go to great lengths to get their message across. If they also know that a direct line to their loved one is not the best way to do that (as in the case of Katie who didn't really believe in that "psychic stuff") they might look for a more receptive messenger, as happened in this tale of psychic telephone tag. Kevin must have known that Mollie would be the perfect person to receive his message and deliver it to his mother. Not only had Mollie also lost a son, she was very open to communication with the world of spirit. His mother, on the other hand, was not only skeptical, but also too emotionally overwrought to receive what he was trying to tell her. By going through Mollie, not only was he able to deliver his message of love to his mother, but, in doing so, he also validated Mollie's own belief that her son, David, had remained a continuing presence in her life. This is one of my favorite stories.

you can communicate also!

While I fully appreciate the fact that I've been given the very special gift of a heightened ability to tune into the vibrations of those in the world of spirit, I also know that every one of you also has the capacity to enhance your own abilities to connect with that world. The one thing you must always remember is that the DPs *want* to make the connection. In fact, it's a major part of their *job* to connect with you. Your job is to open your heart and mind as you learn to listen in this broader sense. If you don't do that, the messages may go unnoticed, and you'll be depriving yourself of the peace and comfort that comes from knowing your departed loved ones are not only "alright" but also still very much connected to you.

It isn't always easy, because you must very deeply want to do it. There may be obstacles in your upbringing or the belief system you were raised with that would make you skeptical or fearful of this kind of contact. No negative energy can enter your realm of being unless you *choose* to allow it in. I don't believe that any loved one who has passed over ever returns with a motive of anger and harm toward us. They are only about love. If you can come to some resolve around those doubts and fears you've been taught, and truly come to believe that you *can* do this, you'll be preparing yourself to hear whatever messages the DPs need to send, even if they bring up issues or thoughts that might be disturbing to *you*. These are only disturbing because you carry or "hang on" to some energy around the issue that hasn't found understanding and resolution. Sometimes this can revolve around the lack of moving into forgiveness for yourself, others present, or those who have passed on. Remember, DPs don't carry resentment, fear, and anger. They have moved on. They are in a state of joy, happiness, and compassion.

If you're willing to become ready, resolved, free of fear, and confirmed in your own belief system, then I'd like to help you by sharing some of the methods I teach people who come to my workshops:

THE PREPARATION

1. First of all, you must let your loved ones know you want to reach them, and when you'll be expecting their contact— sort of like making an appointment for a conference call. So, *make an appointment.* It should be at a time when you're not likely to be disturbed or feeling

anxious about doing other things. Don't, for example, make an appointment for 5:30 on Tuesday if you know your kids or roommates will be around or expecting dinner on the table at 6:30. I've found that early mornings or late evenings are usually best.

2. Secondly, you'll have to commit to doing this for a period of at least seven weeks, so don't start when you know you'll be on a business trip or flying to your best friend's wedding in Boise at this time the week after next.

3. When you've decided on a time, repeat your message once or twice, either aloud or to yourself: "Monday morning, at 7 A.M., I'll be open to receiving communications from . . ." You can ask for a specific person if you like, but be prepared for others who may also show up.

4. Now find a comfortable, quiet place that will be your designated location for the next seven "Mondays" at seven in the morning and place some writing materials at your side.

5. Several minutes before your appointed time, take the phone off the hook, go to your chosen location, and try to prepare

your mind. Make sure you're comfortable—no binding clothing, stomach
neither too full nor too empty—and
allow your body to relax. Try to empty
your mind and tune into your inner ear.
If random thoughts occur, acknowledge
them and let them go. Practicing some
kind of meditation technique—whatever
works for you—may help with this.

6. Imagine yourself surrounded by a white
   light and request permission of God or
   the Higher Power to allow your loved
   ones to come through. Then, seal the light
   and the permission with a prayer, in
   whatever words, directed to whomever
   will give you peace of mind and the
   understanding that whatever happens
   will be for the highest good.

THE MEDITATION OF CONNECTION

Once you feel a sense of safety and protection
from the surrounding light, begin to breathe deeply,
from your diaphragm. As you become more relaxed,
affirm that God or the Higher Power has made this
moment special for you, and feel yourself surrounded
by the light, being lifted gently upward as if in a
balloon, leaving your daily cares and worries behind.

You are being lifted now toward a door above you that opens as you approach and allows you to pass through into a beautiful field of flowers. You feel warm and protected and loved. As you move through the field, you see a gazebo with a bench ahead of you. Someone is waiting for you on the bench. You may or may not see the person clearly, but you approach the bench and sit down next to them. You feel their love touching you.

Even if you don't see or feel the person near you, you know somehow they are near. You hear a word with your inner ear. You may not know immediately what it means, but you know that later you'll understand. If you can see the other person, look into their eyes. If you hear a familiar voice, remain silent and listen. If you feel their touch, be still. This is a special moment that will remain imprinted in your mind.

You'll know when your time is over. I can't explain how; you just will. At that moment, silently tell yourself and your loved one that it's time to go. As you leave the bench, you'll sense that you're once more alone. As you walk back through the field and reenter your balloon of light, you'll know that you can return to this special place again and again. As you are lowered gently, but securely, back through the door, the light will begin to fade and you'll feel yourself returning to your normal state of consciousness. You may not be certain of exactly what has happened, but you'll feel relaxed, secure, and loved in a very special way. Cling to those feelings for a moment.

JOURNALING
YOUR EXPERIENCE

Now, pick up a pen and write down everything you saw or felt, no matter how little or how much. Even if it seems like very little to you at first, you'll be empowering your ongoing relationship. Don't allow the "editor" and "critic" mind/voice to grab hold. Write down anything and everything, whether it makes sense to you at the moment or not or whether it seems significant or not. This information will continue to become clear as you spend time with it.

Even if you think nothing has happened, don't give up. Remember that you're committed for six more weeks, and by practicing your relaxation and visualization techniques, you'll gradually become more comfortable with and open to the process, and the meaning of what you have experienced.

You are already receiving messages whether you can believe it now or not. And don't be surprised if, within the next few days, you begin to "hear" with your higher sense of listening, a message when you least expect it. If it happens so quickly that you're not even sure it occurred at all, let it go. The DPs don't give up easily, and the next message you receive will be easier for you to grasp.

You might also experience some other kind of symbolic connection that lets you know your loved one has received your invitation. As I've said, electronic or mechanical disturbances are among the most common signals the DPs send to remind us of their presence. Or you might notice unusual natural phenomena—flowers blooming out of season or birds appearing when and where they never have before. You might, in fact, have experienced those things at other times and never paid much attention simply because you weren't "tuned in" to their significance.

I would like to give you this quote as you continue to explore connecting and communicating on your own. I rather like it. Claudia Black says, "Trust in yourself. Your perceptions are often far more accurate than you are willing to believe."

trust your dreams

Certainly not every dream in which a DP makes a guest appearance means that your loved one in spirit has paid a nocturnal visit. But, dreams are equally one of the easiest, most common ways the DPs have of contacting us directly.

Why should that be? Anyone who remembers a vivid dream will understand that most dreams have symbolic, rather than purely literal content, and that's because when we're sleeping, the analytical, logical part of our brain also takes a rest, allowing our creative and intuitive faculties free reign. It's that left-brain, right-brain phenomenon again. And since, as I've explained, it's with the intuitive part of our brain that we make contact with those who've passed over, it's during sleep that we are most receptive to receiving these messages.

Dreams are also among the "safest" ways the DPs have of connecting with us. Even people, who are skeptical of the possibility that we can communicate with departed loved ones, seem relatively comfortable dreaming about the dead. Undoubtedly, that's because they're able to rationalize the experience as having dreamt "about" the person, rather than having to accept the fact that they were actually contacted by a loved one in spirit.

Among the most frequently reported dream experiences are those in which a loved one will state that he or she is "not dead" or that he's happy, healthy, and having a good time. That is, after all, the primary message the DPs need to send. As I've said, it's their job to let us know that they're still present, well, and not "dead" at all, in the conventional sense of the word. In any case, isn't that what we'd most like to know about someone we haven't heard from in a while? Don't we want to be reassured that they're safe and doing well, wherever they are?

Here is a story of one person's connection through dreams that I have permission to share:

Dear Suzane,

I am writing you to share my experience using your meditation and connection techniques taught in your seminar. As you know, I lost my mother quite suddenly. She had suffered several seizures over the last couple of years of her life. We, as a family, never felt we got any concrete answers from doctors about what caused these "attacks," we only knew they came on quite suddenly. We had nearly lost her several times as during these attacks she just appeared to start gasping and ultimately would stop breathing. She had a fear of any kind of heart exploration because one of her best friends had died going through such a process, and refused to have anything done of that nature. She was a strong-willed woman with a mind of her own. The only thing we were all left to attribute these episodes to was her heavy smoking. The best we could do was to convince her to stop smoking, which she had done for six months before her death.

We were very close throughout my life. Many times we were able to communicate long distances without words. It was a mental thing that we shared. When we did speak over the phone, we would find we had thought about or had been thinking the same thing at the same time, or done the same thing as the other was doing at the same time. The connection was quite uncanny and provided a lot of fun for us over the years. We would often play a game of "see if you can get this." We could also be together for hours and never say a word.

When she died, as most are in death, I was in disbelief. I never expected that she would depart so soon, at such an early age—she was only 59. Even through the funeral process and months after, I walked around in some kind of denial. I refused to talk about her being "dead." Eventually, as my father, myself, and two brothers began to sort through her personal belongings, I happened on a letter tucked back in the corner of a drawer she had written that was obviously meant to be given to my brothers and

I at some point. Basically what it said was she was tired and exhausted and was hoping to find some peace in her life. She spoke of how she had stuck things out until we were all grown, and that now she wanted us to get on with our lives. She shared that now it was her time, and she planned to move forward with whatever that time presented to find her own happiness. This was heartbreaking. All I wanted was for her to contact me and let me know she was okay. She had had a pretty rough life with my father and I was just hoping she was at last at peace.

I tried everything to make contact. I begged her to give me a sign. When I discovered your work, I thought this might be my answer. To my dismay, she never came through as some of my other family members did in the group sessions. I kept thinking that I didn't want to hear from them. Didn't she understand that I wanted to hear from her? I did your meditation and when at the gazebo on the bench, I could sense her presence—even smell her cologne, but I wanted to "see" her. I needed to see her.

Never one to give up easily, I kept on doing the exercises you suggested. I refused to let go of the belief that I would somehow be contacted. One evening I was feeling particularly saddened by her loss and memory, and as I went to bed I just said a short prayer to the effect that if it is true that we don't just die and cease to exist, I needed some proof from her. That night I got my visit—some one-year after her death.

My mom appeared that night in my dreams. She was dressed in the kind of clothing you would think to see in somewhere like Switzerland. She was dancing in a lush green meadow amidst beautiful surrounding mountains. She had colored ribbons in her hair. She was smiling, singing, and laughing as she ran and danced in the ankle-high grass. She was vibrant, and she told me that she was okay. She asked me to go now and tell my brothers. I awoke the next morning knowing I had had my much-wanted visit. How did I know for sure she was happy and that this was not just a dream? She was of German origin, hence the clothing. Her favorite place she had visited was Switzerland. She had talked about wanting to return many times before her passing. And, she was singing and dancing, which was something as a child, I loved to see and hear her do. The music she was singing to was from her favorite musical. She told me to move on and find my joy because she had found hers. And, that she had visited me many times, and would continue to be around if I needed her.

Sharing this story with you was important. I wanted to share because I believe for sure that if you want contact with someone from the other side, you will get it. You must not give up, and be open to it coming in a way you are not expecting. It took a year for me to make my connection. But it came. I am at peace now. I thank you for all you do for those of us on "this side," and the DPs who desire to connect. Keep the faith!

With much love,
Michelle

So, if you awaken from your dream feeling peaceful and enveloped with intense feelings of love, you have, most likely, experienced a contact with the world of spirit. Trust it. I urge you to write it down as soon as you awaken because the memory, like the memory of all dreams, will be fleeting, and if you don't write it down you won't be able to retain it. But just as you can train yourself, through meditation and practice, to make yourself more open to receiving other kinds of messages, you can also train yourself to have greater access to your dream experiences. You might, for example, practice a meditation just before going to bed, and issue an invitation to your loved one to make contact while you are asleep, just as in Michelle's situation. You might also suggest to yourself that you'll awaken when the contact is over so that you'll remember it. You might not be successful the first time, or every time, but, as with everything in life, you'll get better at it with practice and repetition.

At the same time, however, I need to point out that if your dream makes you fearful or angry or stirs up any kind of negative emotions, those emotions are probably coming from you—from your fear base—because as I've said, the dead people are *never* angry with you, they don't want to make you unhappy or uncomfortable, and they no longer harbor any ill will, whatever may have passed between you while they were alive.

when the messages stop

Once you've been successful in connecting with the DPs, either on your own or with the help of a medium, you'll certainly be wanting the messages to continue, and you'll probably assume that if your loved one "came through" for you once, he or she will undoubtedly do so again. And it's certainly possible that will happen, particularly if you really *need* to continue the contact in order to complete your grieving or come to terms with some aspect of your relationship that was unfinished on this plane. This is often true when a parent has lost a child, which is without a doubt one of the most devastating losses anyone can sustain. Or you may find that you just sense a presence on special occasions, such as holidays, birthdays, and anniversaries, which would be your loved one's way of letting you know that he or she knows that it's a special day and that he's still aware of what's happening in your life. But it's also possible that after one or two contacts, your DP won't be there for you again.

I don't know exactly why this happens, but I do know that this also happens for a reason. Perhaps your loved one just needed to assure you that he loved you and was still a presence in your life, and, having delivered this message, there was no more for him to say. Or perhaps he or she needed to move on with his own soul's growth and evolution, just as you now need to let go and move on with your own. You have to remember that just as you have to move forward, the DPs, too, have work they must complete.

You will no doubt be disappointed if your contacts are cut off, but you shouldn't be disillusioned. Remember that before you began these contacts, you gave yourself over to the Higher Power and avowed that you were acting for the highest good. It's simply not up to you to decide when that *good* has been accomplished.

chapter two

understanding
the afterlife

death is a new beginning

O ver the years, and with growing familiarity, I've shared with you that I have come to think of those folks living on that other plane as members of the *Dead People's Society*, or, as you might know by now if you have read any of my other books or attended one of my seminars, I call them with both respect and affection, DPs. And, I speak of their existence as a "society" because, in fact, the Afterlife is not lived in isolation but in a *society of souls*, just as we on this plane are members of a society living in relationship to one another.

One of the greatest misconceptions people can have about death is to think of it as an ending. While it may be the conclusion of one specific phase of the soul's journey, death is just as surely the beginning of the next. Death, for those of us who are remaining here, only marks the end of one phase of our relationship with the one who's passed over. It is also the beginning of another—if we desire it to be—because the Soul never dies, and neither does the relationship between those who are on this plane and those on the other side.

If there's one thing I've learned—and have come to accept unequivocally—during the course of my work, and through thousands of conversations with those who have passed over, it's that the concept of "death" doesn't exist as most people think of it. It's simply another phase of transition in the evolution of our soul's ongoing existence and quest for growth, *lived*, at least temporarily, on another plane. If it were a play, it would be the next act. If it were a book, it would be the next chapter. It's metaphorically like throwing a pebble into the water and watching the ripple effect that is created. As with our soul's growth, it just keeps rippling outward ad infinitum. Never-ending. Ever expanding.

love:
the bond that never ends

Until we learn to overcome our skepticism, and open ourselves to the possibility of life after death, we will remain unaware of the continuous signs that are given to us constantly that those relationships still exist. For those who have passed, there is no doubt. And, they are passionate about letting us know. Many times, during readings or séances, one of the DPs will tell me that he or she has been in contact with his or her *living* loved one on a regular basis, and when I pass that information along, more often than not, the person has been unaware of those contacts.

Just as physicists know for a scientific fact that energy never dies, I know, as a fact, that the undying energy of love is what binds us to our loved ones who have passed. Neither the DPs nor my clients ever let me forget that. We all know the strength of love. There isn't one of us that have not experienced the power of love in some way or another. It has the ability to produce complete healing as strongly as it does total annihilation. This fact was brought home to me again, quite powerfully, when a man at one of my tour seminars had this experience:

> I attended one of Suzane's seminars in the Southwest and was not quite sure why I was going, or what I was expecting. My wife of 47 years had died some six months ago and I had been consumed not only with grief but also with an overwhelming

sense of guilt. It was to be a full-on weekend with Suzane in a group situation that I was not sure I was ready to go through. I had never been one to be very enthused about these "group things." Yet, something was drawing me there after hearing about her through some supportive and concerned friends. I must admit that I was quite skeptical, although I had come to a point personally that I knew I must find some sort of relief from this ongoing pain.

Virginia, my wife, had suffered a stroke and had been in a coma for about six weeks before her death. She had been a beautifully strong and loving person. Everyone who knew her adored her love of life and giving spirit. It had been extremely hard for me over the weeks before her passing to watch her lying in the hospital so lifeless. I kept thinking over and over how could this be happening to this wonderful woman who I loved so dearly. I was at the point of exhaustion from the constant vigil, and yet, I was afraid to be away from her for any length of time.

Finally one evening, feeling totally depleted, I decided I would leave the hospital and go to sleep in our home, our bed. I remember that it seemed like it took me hours to make this simple decision. From the doctor's information earlier in the day, it looked quite hopeless that there would be any chance of her recovering and coming back to full capacity. I was so torn by these words. I felt utterly powerless to do anything for this woman I had loved for so long. In the hour that it took me to bring myself to leave, I remember talking to Virgie and telling her how much I loved her. I wanted to make sure she could hear that. At least, I hoped she could hear that. Someone had told me that people in comas quite often could hear those speaking to them. I also was surprised to hear myself saying that it was okay if she wanted to "move on". I knew this formerly vibrant woman would not want to remain if it were to be in this state. We had discussed this at times before.

When I got home that evening, I took a warm shower and climbed into bed. I remember turning toward her side of the bed and just for a moment thought I could smell the fragrance of her favorite body powder fill the air. I smiled and drifted off to sleep. The next thing I knew the phone woke me with its ringing. At first, I wondered why Virgie hadn't answered it. She was the lighter sleeper. Then I rose up with a start. It was the hospital calling to tell me that she had passed. I guess I really knew it before I even picked up the phone.

In the months since, I had tried to move through my grief as best I could. The underlying difficulty had been in that I told her it was okay to go, and she went. So many times I have thought that if I just had not done that, she might still be around. Maybe I was wrong. I have lived with quite a bit of guilt wondering if I did right.

So, here I am in Suzane's seminar and before I knew it she is saying there is this woman present, and walked toward my area of the room. She said she was getting a powder-like fragrance and a "V" sound coming through. Then she looked right at me and said that it was my wife and she was here to let me know that I had done the right thing in letting her go and that she was well, happy, and loved me. She also thanked me for staying by her side while she was in the coma, and giving her permission to let go. The tears began to roll down my cheeks. I knew it was Virgie. I felt immense relief and now knew I could begin to move on in my life. She would be there.

Thank you, God. Thank you, Virgie. Thank you, Suzane.

In this case, Virgie knew she needed to come back and help her husband release so *he* could move on. Never doubt the power of love. How could you after something like this?

we never pass over alone

A second misconception many people have about death is that it's a lonely passing for the soul crossing over. But I know from experience, because the DPs have told me, that we never die alone. We never make the transition from body back to spirit without some help from the other side. Isolation and disconnection are not part of the universal "master plan." Rather, we are always met and helped over to the other side by a family member or other loved one who eases the shock of the journey and helps us adjust to life on a different plane.

I'm invariably told by the DPs that they've been met and brought over by someone who passed before them.

Although, as I'll explain further in just a bit, members of a "nuclear family" don't necessarily remain together after death, they are still very much a family, and they live in society with others, just as we do here on earth. So the bottom line is that sometimes it may be only one DP who comes to help the departed over, but more often it will be more than one.

What we all need to understand is that our departed loved one is never alone and neither are we. It's the job of souls who have gone before to ease the passage of those who go after them. It's also the job of those who have passed to maintain their contact with us here in order to help us work through our grief, achieve resolution, and move on with the rest of our journey.

Here is an amazing story that affirms my statement that we never cross over alone:

> There was a woman, Daria, who came to one of my séances. A group of about eight people were in attendance that evening. I had been delivering messages for about half an hour when all of a sudden two large dogs appeared and walked over by her. With them, I saw a very handsome young man and he wanted his presence to be known by this woman. I spoke, acknowledging that he was there behind her with the dogs. I told her I was feeling uncomfortably warm and said that the young man's name began with or had something like a "D" or "L" or "DL."

Her eyes widened as she looked at me. I asked if she recognized who this might be. "Daniel," she said and burst into tears. I told her that Daniel wanted her to know he was there, he loved her, and he was fine, happy, and well. It was important for him that she knew the two dogs were there also.

After a few moments, Daria was able to compose herself and began to share with the group her story. It seems that Daniel was 24 years old and lived in another city. He was her favorite son and had decided to move to a different location in order to have a better opportunity for his chosen field of work. He had obtained a small old house and therefore took along his two beloved pet boxers to live with him and provide company.

One night as Daniel slept, due to faulty wiring and a space heater, the old house caught fire and burned to the ground. Neither Daniel nor the dogs made it out. This had been a horrifying loss for Daria. Tragic and sudden. No opportunity for closure. This being her favorite child, she had had a terrible time moving past the grief. She often wondered how it must have been for him to die that way and wondered if he had struggled, or even awakened. The only thing she knew was that the firefighters had told her about something they thought was unusual when they were finally able to recover the body.

When they began clearing their way through the rubble, at first they thought they had only found two dogs huddled together, they were so badly burned. Yet, as they began to pull them away, underneath they found Daniel's body. It appeared the dogs had covered him trying to protect him. They could have tried to get away but for some reason they stayed. Now they were here with Daniel to let his mom know he was okay, and not alone. That she could move on.

Now who's to say whether Daniel or the dogs passed over first, and who might have helped them all over. What this story confirms for me is that we are *never* alone, whether it is in the dying process or the crossing over process.

I don't know about you, but this gives me some comfort beyond just being a touching and heart-warming story. It made me think about when multiple deaths happen, and we have surely experienced that magnified recently with the tragic events of September 11, here in the United States. This was a massive passing over that none of us will ever forget. What came to mind is that quite possibly there were many of those that died who were helping the others over. It's like this vision of many hands reaching out to create a bridge to the other side.

That, my friends, warms my heart when I try to keep in mind that everything happens for a reason. It's hard to understand something so senseless. It's challenging to remember that each soul has its path and plan. And yet, I know it does. I believe that their deaths would be without purpose if we didn't take time to try and have some understanding of what the message of such a huge loss was to mean to us. I have taken that time. I hope you have, too.

and it doesn't stop with physical death

Because the Soul never dies, it is on an ongoing journey, in both this life and the Afterlife—a journey of growth and discovery. We are all in this life for a purpose—whether or not we're aware of it—and that purpose is to learn, to accomplish what each soul has chosen as its program, and that could mean anything. Basically, it's whatever our souls need to learn. It might be patience or self-reliance or dealing with loss or compassion. Each soul has a different program and no two souls need to learn or accomplish exactly the same thing. The Soul's path is to grow, and each path is unique for each soul. Incarnating into a human body provides a level of learning that cannot be accomplished on any other dimension. If we haven't completed the purpose of our program on this plane, we'll just continue it after we pass over until it's time for the soul to return, and move on into another physical body. There are certain lessons that are to be learned only through the human existence. It's like, on some level, a graduate course.

That's one of the main reasons why our loved ones don't really *leave* us when they pass over. Because they love us—and they do love us, make no mistake about that—it's not only their duty but also their wish to help us move on with *our* own journey. They know that in order to do that we have to come to some kind of resolution regarding their death. It's part of the learning. And by letting us know they're okay—happy and without pain—they're telling us not only that we don't have to worry about them but also that we don't have to mourn their passing because they're really still with us. A perfect example of the lengths to which the DPs will go to help us achieve resolution occurred when a client came to see me while she was pregnant with twins.

> While on the discussion of her impending deliveries, I told my client I was picking up a set of twins who had passed, but the woman assured me that there were no other twins in her family, and, clearly, the twins she was carrying were very much alive. After our meeting, my client asked her mother if she knew of any other twins in the family, but her mother adamantly denied any such knowledge.
>
> After she gave birth, the woman came to see me a second time, and once more I picked up the twins who were in spirit. All I could tell her was that they were very much there, and absolutely insistent that they belonged to her. Again, she confirmed that her twin babies

were very much alive, and returned once again to her mother seeking validation, asking if she might somehow have forgotten these twins, perhaps from a previous generation.

At that point her mother broke down in tears and confessed that before my client's birth, she'd given birth to a set of twins who had died. She told her daughter that she'd never been able to bring herself to speak of them because the experience had been so painful for her.

Not only was the mystery solved, but my client was immediately certain that her own twins were, in some way, sent to "replace" the twins her mother had lost. She sensed that their birth would allow her mother the opportunity to arrive at some sense of completion and resolution of her long-held sorrow. And, in addition, she and her mother would be able to share a level of intimacy they'd been unable to enjoy so long as her mother had been unable to share her secret.

In this instance, my client wasn't even aware that there *was* an issue to be resolved between her and her mother, but because she was open to the possibility of a continuum of life after death, and because her siblings on the other side understood that she'd be receptive to their message, they were able to move one step farther on the path of growth and understanding. Being able to help people do that is one of the greatest rewards my gift has been able to give me over and over again.

Sometimes, however, we're unable to complete all the lessons we're supposed to while we're still on this plane, and when that happens, our learning and growth will have to continue in the Afterlife. As I've said, no one passes alone from this plane to the next. There's always a relative or loved one there to help us over, but the Afterlife isn't necessarily one big ongoing family reunion. Depending on what it is that individual souls have to learn, families or loved ones don't necessarily remain together once they've passed. Although there are other instances when souls, for whatever reason, *need* to find one another on the other side, and in those cases, they always do, because it's part of their program.

They're there, often in a group, when we need to contact them, and most often more than one family member will make himself known to help validate or provide identifying information, but otherwise, their soul's journey might take them in different directions. Not every soul needs to learn the same lesson or do the same work, that only makes sense. Sometimes that means families are split up—just as they are in this life.

Consider what happens when two people marry young, before they've both fully matured. Sometimes they grow together and remain with one another throughout a long life. But quite often, they find that they grow apart and need to move in separate directions. When that happens, they might continue to love one another, and they will always be connected to one another—and to other members of the family they "married into"—by the bond the marriage created, but they don't necessarily continue to live together. And the same thing happens in the spirit realm. The Soul's journey is all about growth, and it's difficult, if not impossible, to grow if we don't ever venture off on our own and move beyond the familiarity of our "comfort zone."

If you think of it in terms of a job—and remember that every soul has a program that might easily be compared to its job—you'll understand that if you continue to do exactly the same work year after year, not only will you never learn new skills but you'll also become bored and stagnant in what you're doing. Have you heard the definition of insanity is doing the same things over and over, time and again, and expecting different results? (I give exception to those of us that work as mediums—we're hopefully learning more and more by what we are doing over and over—we are the "lifers.") In order to grow and learn, in the Afterlife as well as in this life, you have to move on, move out, and take risks.

That's why even those who pass as young children continue to grow and mature in the Afterlife. When they make contact with you on this plane, they'll always be recognizable, because they'll provide you with the validating information you need. But very often when a child comes through for me, they'll give their present age, not the age they were when they passed. Then, when I ask the parents what age their child was when they passed, the difference will coincide exactly with the number of years since his or her death.

when it's time to return

If the Soul never dies and the purpose of it's continuing journey is learning and growth, there will come a time for that journey to continue on this plane. Herein we find the purpose of reincarnation. At the completion of each earthly life, and during the between life, either our soul will have learned all it needs to move on to the next level of growth, or it will have learned all it can *without* a physical body. In either case, a time will come for each soul to reincarnate and return to this life.

We are all, as I've said, here for a purpose. We all, in our physical bodies, represent just one stop on our soul's everlasting journey; and we are all who we are because each soul has chosen a particular path to learning and growth. As you read on and learn more about what I've come to call *The Soul Program*, you'll understand more of why I know that everything happens for a reason, there are no accidents in life, and coincidences are just God's way of remaining anonymous. For now, let me simply assure you that you, too, are here for a purpose, and making contact with those who have passed is one means of helping you to discover what your own purpose might be.

When I tell that to people, they're sometimes concerned that their loved one will reincarnate and return to this plane before they've had a chance to contact him or her. But that really never happens, for the simple reason that the DPs do know what's happening on this plane, and it's their *job* to be there when you need them. It's part of *their* program to help you fulfill yours, and so they won't—in fact they can't—desert you while they know they're still needed. Besides, it usually takes five generations before a specific soul reincarnates. This is not a hardened rule, as with anything there are exceptions. So, please—and I know we quite often only hear what we want to hear— I don't want you going off saying that Suzane said you could *only* reincarnate every five generations. No, what I am saying is that it is the usual rule, but if someone *needs* to connect with a loved one on this side or the other side, the DPs will do all they can to provide. I spoke of this once in a seminar and afterwards a gentleman, who worked in cemeteries, came to me and said that the "five generation thing" made sense to him. He told that it was quite common among those who worked in this environment to notice that after about five generations, the families stopped visiting the gravesite. I did not know that, did you?

But if, on the other hand, they know they've done their job by letting you know that they love you and are still very much part of your life, they might not contact you again because they know that what you need is to move past your dependency on them in order to be able to continue your own journey. That's why some people might receive only a single message or make only a single contact with a loved one in spirit while others continue to "remain in touch" more frequently and for a much longer time. The DPs know what we need from them even if we sometimes don't, and they always have our best interests at heart.

The most important thing for each one of us to remember is that, although they may have moved on to another plane, our loved ones have not really left us. They still care about us, and they want to help us. Although we won't physically be able to put our arms around them and give them a hug, we can still make contact with them and let them know we love them, too. We still have a chance to say things we might have failed to convey to them in life, and we can still resolve issues that were left unresolved before they moved on. What we always need to keep in mind, though, is that while *we* may need to seek resolution, our loved ones do not. Even if they were disappointed, angry, jealous, or in any other way less than happy with us in life, those feelings were left behind when they passed, and while they will do all that they can to help us come to terms with our own feelings, all they feel for us now is love.

chapter three

the boundary
program explained

When I was much younger and didn't yet understand my affinity for communicating with the DPs, which I now appreciate as a special gift that's been bestowed on me by God, I found that members of the Dead People's Society were making themselves known whether I thought I wanted them to or not. Sometimes it was embarrassing; sometimes other people thought I was nuts; and sometimes even I thought I was nuts. For a long time, I kept trying to ignore them, hoping that they'd "give up" and go call on someone else. I now realize, of course, that they were simply taking advantage of my receptive "open line" to try to make me understand a calling I hadn't yet acknowledged even to myself. But I also understand that if my psychic phone line hadn't been ready to receive their calls, they wouldn't have come through. Because I wasn't ready, they didn't make themselves clear. That's the basic premise of The Boundary Program.

The Boundary Program is a protocol based on loving respect that means no one on this plane or in spirit can enter another's vibration without his or her permission. For many people, I think the notion that the DPs can contact us, or we them, is not only weird but a little frightening, particularly if the relationship between the living and the person who has passed was less than completely warm and loving. And part of that fear, I believe, stems from the mistaken notion that the dead folks are "spying" on us from the other side—that they can actually "see" everything we're doing here on earth at all times.

Who, after all would want their meddling mother-in-law checking up on their housekeeping skills from the beyond, or their overprotective father passing judgment on their current relationships? Nor are our parents watching us having sex (and with whom and how), or watching us in the bathroom to make sure we "clean" ourselves appropriately. Really, now! That would, indeed, be pretty scary for anyone, but it just doesn't happen that way. If it did, I'd be walking around every day bombarded by "messages"

I didn't really understand but was supposed to deliver to people I didn't even know.

Every person I met would assume I was "reading their mind" or receiving communications from their loved ones on the other side. People would be afraid of me (with good reason) and I'd probably go mad, which is exactly what I sometimes thought was happening in the early days when I didn't really understand how the system worked. But now that I do, I'm able to tune in and out of the DPs vibrations, to let them know when, as they used to say in polite society, I'm "receiving," and when I'm "not at home to visitors." And the DPs respect that with me, as they do with everyone on this plane.

let them know you're receptive

In order to receive messages from our loved ones in spirit, we have to be mentally and emotionally open and prepared to learn what they have to tell us. Well, at least, we have to listen. It's also up to us to let them know when we are ready to welcome their communication. To facilitate communication, you can, of course, make an appointment with the DPs in your life as we learned about in the section called *You Can Communicate Also!* This way, they'll know when and where you're waiting to hear from them. But even if you don't do that, they'll be able to pick up from your vibrations, whether or not you're ready to receive their messages. Sometimes, if you're still in mourning, if the death of your loved one has been particularly traumatic, or if you're still feeling angry or confused about his or her death, you may want to communicate, but still have some reservations.

The DPs take their cues from you about contact, and if you happen to still be traumatized and in emotional turmoil, they know you are too clouded for them to get through. Actually, no one can get through when someone is in that state. For the DPs, taking the cues from you is part of The Boundary Program and they will hold back until they feel you are clearer and in a place of calm. In this case, it's up to you to let your DP know by sending a mental message when you are ready or when you are not. *I do want to hear from you, but I'm not really emotionally prepared right now, or I am ready to hear from you.*

This reminds me of a mother in one seminar, who's daughter slept in the departed grandfather's room and was visited by him on a regular basis. She told her mother this and also that she was a bit frightened by his visits. The mother asked me what to say to her. My reply was that it was okay to tell her daughter to say to the grandfather that she appreciated him coming but it wasn't the right time. Could he come some other time when she was more comfortable with the visits? In this case, the mom didn't want to stop the possible gift this young girl was developing, but wanted her to feel safe now, and in control.

The DP will respect your wishes, because they're connected to you by love, but it's also their duty to let you know that things are good, and that they still love you, and so quite often they may go through another person to send their message. Usually that would be another family member, but sometimes a DP might also take advantage of the good will and receptivity of a total stranger, as was the case at one of my recent séances. This unexpected visit provided one of the most moving experiences of the entire afternoon—one that even those who weren't directly involved could sense was particularly emotional for the woman who received the message:

> A woman, Rita, had come to the séance with her sister, and they'd both received and welcomed several clear acknowledgments from various members of their family. And then, near the end, a woman came through, showing me very insistently a candle that had been lit, she indicated, as a welcome. Sure, a candle. Practically everyone in the room could think of some occasion on which a candle had been significant, but no one seemed to think this particular candle had any real significance for them. No one was claiming the message until Rita remembered that she'd quite recently been to the funeral of a friend's mother at which candles were lit. That was exactly the connection the woman in spirit had been trying to make. She let it be known that she wanted Rita to tell both her daughter and her grandson that she'd come through,

and that she was now well and no longer in pain. She said she'd stayed on this plane longer than she would have wished, that she was much more cognizant at the end of what was going on than her daughter had thought, and that she was happy to be where she was. She indicated that she'd been brought over by her husband, who'd passed before her, and she acknowledged a silver serving platter of hers that her daughter had given to Rita after her passing.

By the time the connection was over, Rita was in tears, and the emotion in the room was palpable. Perhaps it was because the message was so unexpected or because it was so filled with love, but it was definitely one of the more astonishing connections made that day.

Because the passing was so recent and the daughter's emotions were still so raw, Rita didn't want to give her the information directly, but she did very much want to fulfill the mother's request, so she called her friend's husband and told him what had happened. She suggested that he wait to pass the message on until he felt his wife was ready to receive it, and she let him know that she'd also let him and his wife listen to the tape she'd made of the session whenever they wanted to do that.

The DPs are extremely sensitive to the feelings of those they've left on this plane, but once you've put yourself in a situation that lets them know you're open to hearing from them (as Rita did that day simply by being at a séance), they absolutely *will* respond because they love you and it's their duty to let you know that.

The messages you receive, however, may not be exactly the ones you were waiting for, or expecting. Listen to them. Sometimes their message is one you *should* hear, even if you think you don't want to.

Remember, too, that whatever our preconceived notion of how they should talk to us or what we might want them to say, our loved ones might have an agenda that's different from our own. They're in a different place now—both literally and figuratively, and what seems important to you may no longer be so important to them—or maybe they just don't want to discuss it.

When we're dealing with the living, we understand that not everyone is willing or able to communicate as openly as we might wish. Not everyone is equally capable of expressing their feelings. Maybe your mother was very warm and open while your father was more "buttoned up." That doesn't mean your father loved you any the less; it just means he kept things to himself. In most families, there are many things that simply go unsaid. And yet, when someone dies, we expect those dynamics to change. They do, in fact, change at least to the extent that the DPs will carry out their responsibility for letting us know they're coming through, but we seem to expect them not only to come through but also to tell us whatever it is we want to hear in the way we want to hear it. That doesn't always happen in life, and there's no reason for us to expect that it's always going to happen after death.

Sometimes we may not even be aware that we're opening the door or issuing an invitation for our loved ones in spirit to pay us a visit, and then the response we receive may be more than a little surprising. It could, in fact, be just the "coincidence" that convinces an adamant skeptic that there's something beyond chance at work in his or her life.

Just such a skeptic phoned in to a radio broadcast I was doing not to long ago to tell me the story of his own mind-opening experience:

The gentleman on the call-in began to share that he had been installing a ceiling fan in his new apartment. His friend, who was there to help him, asked where he'd learned such a skill, and he told his friend that his father, who had been an electrician, had taught him. So he'd been talking about his father, and, no doubt, thinking that if only he'd been there to help, the job would have gone much faster. Then, just as he was about to get it done, he realized he was missing two screws that were essential for holding the fan in place. Muttering under his breath about how no job is ever as easy as you thought it would be, he got down from his ladder and went to the toolbox that had been left to him by his father to see if he could find two screws that might work. As he fingered through the toolbox, right there on top, he found two gleaming green screws almost glowingly standing out from everything else. Are you surprised that they were exactly the right size? Totally flabbergasted now, he grabbed the screws and finished hanging the fan as he gave a chuckle.

Even my skeptical caller had to admit that the odds of his finding two screws of exactly the right size, and that they would be a different color from any of the other screws in the box, were way beyond the bounds of what anyone could call coincidence. Sometimes the help we get from the DPs can be of a very practical nature!

Sometimes we ask for something, and when we get it, we're too blind or too foolish or too stubborn to accept it. That happened to me many years ago when I was very young, very poor, and, I guess, less understanding of how these things work than I am now. In any case, I was sitting in my apartment one day feeling so hungry, just wishing I could afford the ingredients to make a bowl of vegetable stew. That's all I wanted, and I remember saying out loud to God, "All I want is a bowl of stew. Is that so much to ask? Am I such a bad person?" And then, about 20 minutes later, a friend called to invite me out to dinner as a way of saying thank you for something I'd done to help her out with a problem. And what do you think I did? "Oh, that's okay, you don't have to do that." I declined! I just got what I'd wanted—something to eat—and I threw it away because it didn't come exactly the way I'd wanted it.

We think we're supposed to get information the way we want it; we even decide what kind of information we want and how we're supposed to get it. But that's not always the way it happens. I guess on that day I was being told I wasn't such a bad person, and I could have my stew if I wanted it, but I simply couldn't see that at the time because it didn't step right up and bite me on the nose. I urge you to try to be more alert and less stubborn than I was, to recognize when you've received something you asked for—even if it doesn't arrive exactly as you imagined it would (or should)—and not to be so stubborn that you refuse it.

sometimes they can't tell you because they love you

There may, however, be times when we very much want a particular kind of help or piece of information from a DP that he or she, because of the protocols of The Boundary Program, is not at liberty to pass on. The DPs can't, for example, pass on information that would interfere with our Karmic progression by changing the course of our soul's journey here on earth.

While it's their job to help you work through and resolve your grief so that you can move on with your life, they can't interrupt or redirect the path you've chosen because that would be denying your freedom of choice (which I'll be discussing further in the following chapter) and preventing you from learning the lessons you're here to learn that would mean hurting rather than helping you. Again, it's all about love.

So, when I'm asked by a client whether a DP can tell her what's going to happen in her future, I can only respond: He probably knows the answer, but he may not be able to communicate it to you. If, for example, you were to ask your mother now in spirit, "Should I marry George?" or "Should I quit my job?" you probably wouldn't get an answer because that decision is yours to make—it's one of the lessons you need to learn. And if you do marry George, and he turns out to be a jerk, or quit your job and wind up in one that's even worse, well, those are lessons, too.

But the DPs do love you, which means they want to help you as much as they can. So they may put a particular person or circumstance in your path—anonymously, of course—and it will then be up to you to take advantage of the opportunity. Very often, for example, when a parent dies, a survivor might, coincidentally, just happen to "meet someone" shortly thereafter, and then, in a session, the parent will let me know that he or she has "pulled the strings" to insure that meeting would occur. Putting a person or circumstance in your path is a way of helping you to move on with your life—if you are alert enough to see the opportunity and choose to take advantage of it. Think of the dead folks as your guardian angels, because, although not all guardian angels are dead people connected to you, many of them are, and their job is to do what's best for you. If you're in need, and you ask for help, you'll get it from those on the other side.

They're always there for you, and they want you to know that. That's why, on certain occasions, such as holidays, many people say they "feel the presence" of a loved one, or they might receive a message that, in retrospect, they realize came from a particular person on the other side. This is especially true at events that mark a significant turning point in one's life. Very often, for example, a bride or groom will sense that his or her parent, in spirit, was present during the ceremony.

they respect you because they love you

The Boundary Program, as I said, is based on respect—for your feelings and for your privacy. For that reason, the DPs won't give you information in the presence of other people that might damage your relationships with those who are still living.

Not too long ago, a woman came to me accompanied by her daughter and her brother, who happened to be a priest. The woman's husband had passed and she wanted to give her daughter the opportunity to make a connection with him. From the moment they entered the room, I sensed that the woman's brother was quite resistant to what we were going to be doing, and he was acting altogether quite strangely. At the time, I simply attributed his behavior to the fact that he was a priest and that his religious calling was preventing him from being open to the possibility of after-death communication, as is sadly true for many people of the cloth.

The woman's husband did come through that day. Both she and her brother acknowledged the information they were receiving with "yes" or "no" answers, but they were otherwise much less forthcoming than most people would have been, particularly in a private session. Usually people not only acknowledge that they understand a message, they are eager to let me know why and in what way it's significant for them—but not these two.

Only later did I find out, because the woman shared the information with me that her brother and her husband had not gotten along, and that her daughter had been unaware of the animosity between them. Her brother, she said, had been afraid that her husband might say something that would let his niece know their relationship had been difficult, and that's why he'd been behaving so strangely.

Of course, the father did not make his daughter privy to what was, after all, a private matter between him and his brother-in-law. He was well aware of the family dynamics, and he wouldn't have allowed his own feelings to damage the relationship between his daughter and her uncle. That's part of what The Boundary Program is all about. Had this woman shared her information with me in advance, I could have reassured her on that score. As it is, I wondered why her brother had come at all, but I suspect he'd have been just as nervous about *not* hearing what was said as he was about possibly hearing it.

In séances and seminars, where larger groups of people, most of them strangers to one another, are involved, the privacy issue becomes even more relevant than it is in private readings. In group situations, after all, it's almost as if one were being asked to strip naked in public—and, in fact, one's emotions are often laid bare in front of the entire room. That's one of the reasons, as I've said, that I always dim the lights during all sessions. But again, the protocol of respect is always at work—at least on the part of the DPs. The living, sad to say, are not always so respectful.

After a group séance held in my home a year or so ago, one of the participants, a woman named Harriet, informed me that she'd been to see me several years earlier for a private reading. I, of course, had no recollection of what had taken place, both because I see so many people and because, as I've indicated, I almost never remember what's taken place unless I'm reminded of it or told about it after the fact.

During the séance, Harriet received many acknowledgments and messages from loved ones who'd passed, including a connection made by her brother, who asked her to please assure their parents that he was fine, and who acknowledged that his passing had been difficult for the family. I sensed damage to the head and upper body and I knew that he'd gone quickly, but he didn't pass on anything more specific about the way he'd died.

Afterwards, Harriet told me that her brother had shot himself, and she said that in our earlier private reading, I'd described his manner of death so accurately and startlingly that she'd been, as she put it, "astonished." And she was wondering why the information he'd given during the séance had been so much less specific.

I told her there were two possibilities. The first was that, since he'd already come through for her before, and he knew she was aware of his continuing connection, he didn't feel the need to do anything more on this occasion than to acknowledge that he was still there. Or, very likely he was protecting her privacy by not revealing the specifics of his death in front of a roomful of people with whom she might not have wanted to share that information. There's always a reason, whether we understand it or not, for what the DPs do or don't convey to us.

when your loved one was murdered

Obviously, any kind of violent death is traumatic, not only to the survivors but also to the person who has passed. When it's a case of murder, the ramifications can be extremely difficult for both. The two things most people want to know about their loved ones, whose death resulted from that kind of violence, are whether the victim was in pain and also "whodunit."

Violent death can complicate communication because it might have been so sudden or so shocking that the DP doesn't yet realize he's dead. Since communication is dependent upon the continuation of consciousness, I can't actually reach a person who doesn't yet know he's passed over. But in these cases, I will usually receive a message from someone close to the victim, perhaps the person who helped him over, to let the family know their loved one isn't alone and that he's "okay."

"Whodunit," however, can be a more complicated question, one whose answer is very often governed by the protocols of The Boundary Program. There may be circumstances, for example, when the DP feels he'd be putting you, the living, in danger by revealing that information, and in those cases, he simply won't be able to provide it. I experienced that protocol at work several years ago, when a brother and sister came to me wanting to contact their mother, who'd been murdered.

The mother, they told me, had answered her front door one day, and whoever was on the other side had shot her point-blank in the head. Her children had been at home but hadn't seen the perpetrator. Now they wanted their mother to tell them who had killed her. The mother did make contact during our session and gave enough validating information so that her children were certain it was really she, but she wouldn't/couldn't/didn't let me know who the murderer was. In this case, I had to explain to the children, it simply wasn't meant to be, and, personally, I'm certain she knew (or believed) that their ignorance was the only thing protecting her children from being in danger themselves.

On another occasion, however, the outcome was quite different. In this case, my friend's brother had disappeared, and she asked me to try to find out what had happened to him. My friend was fairly certain he was dead, although no body had been found. Although locating bodies or helping with crime investigations is not something I normally do, for a variety of reasons that I'll discuss further in a minute, I wanted to help my friend. I was able to "see" her brother's body in the trunk of a car, and I saw that the car was near water. I couldn't determine if the body was still in the trunk, but I did know the man was dead, and I even picked up the name of the murderer, who, as it turned out, was someone his sister knew as well. In this instance, I *was* allowed to receive the information, because the DP thought it would be appropriate to tell me.

Sometimes, in fact, the victim is almost *insistent* on providing information. A woman came to see me with her two sons seeking to contact her ex-husband, who had moved away to the South and remarried some time before. He had recently disappeared. At the time, there was no proof that he was even dead, and, in fact, his new wife insisted he'd simply "taken off." She even sent his sons a picture of the pond he'd been building at the time. The father had been so proud of it, and she thought the sons would want to see it. The older son was, nevertheless, certain his father was dead. Sure enough, the man showed up almost immediately, announcing vehemently that his second wife and her boyfriend had murdered him. He also kept mentioning "the pond," and his insistence must have tweaked the older son's suspicion, because he asked the police in the town where his father had been living to investigate further, and when they did, they found that he'd actually been buried in that pond.

These are certainly extreme, not to mention violent, examples of The Boundary Program at work, but they should help you to understand that it's a protocol meant for our protection and that it's an example of the ways our loved ones continue to do what's best for us even after they've passed over.

That protective protocol can have even broader ramifications, however, with relation to a medium's ability to contact the dead. Very often, if we can't give the living the information they're seeking, they use what they perceive to be a failure on our part to invalidate any other information we might have been able to provide. What these people don't understand, however, is that the DPs might be protecting *us* (the mediums) as much as they're protecting their living loved ones.

What if we did, in effect, accuse someone of murder? Who would believe us? Certainly our information couldn't be used as evidence in a court of law, and we could easily be threatened with a libel suit by whomever we'd named. The DPs know that, and they might well decide that it would be too much of a risk for *us* to pass on that kind of information.

Or it just might be that the DP has moved past his cause of death and is now concerned with whatever further work his soul has to complete in order to move on in its journey. We can't simply assume that our agenda is the same as that of the one who has passed.

Recently, with so much publicity being given to the abduction of children, I keep being asked (none-too-politely, I might add) why, if I'm "so good," I can't find all these missing children. Frankly, I'm tired of being accused of "copping out" or somehow failing to do my job. My answer to these people is always the same: If you've never worked with anyone in my field, how can you possibly know how mediums work? And, furthermore, if we *had* access to information about every kind of crime, there would be no free will, no individual choice in life, as we know it.

Mediums are "psychic," certainly, but not all psychics are mediums. And, since psychics do sometimes assist in police investigations, I should point out the difference between the way they gather information and the way we mediums work. It's true that we're both tapping into the same mind consciousness source system, but psychics don't connect directly with the person who has passed. They work with evidential information, and they've trained themselves to receive specific details related to a particular case. They might help to lead the investigators to a particular location or to the weapon itself, but they don't connect directly with the victim in order to discover who the perpetrator was.

In addition, even psychics most often work with small town police departments where there is less media attention and political pressure than in big city or high profile cases. The family of the victim, rather than the police themselves, who then relay the information they receive from the psychic to the proper authorities, often contacts them. When the glare of publicity is on a case, however, police would be much less likely to admit they were so "stumped" as to have consulted a psychic. So, again, before people accuse me and my colleagues of somehow shirking our civic duty, I wish they would give some serious thought to the larger ramifications of what it is they're asking of us.

my role in the boundary program

Although it's up to the DPs, not me, to decide what messages or information they want to deliver to their loved ones, I believe that I, too, have certain responsibilities as the medium through which they communicate. I can only repeat that I consider my ability a gift from the Higher Power, and I believe that I must cherish that gift and treat it as the blessing I know it to be. And because the people who come to me are so dependent upon me for interpreting both the nature and content of the messages I receive, I believe it's my duty to be particularly vigilant and circumspect about how and what I tell them.

In some instances a DP might relay to me in any number of ways that the sitter or someone close to him or her is soon to pass over. Although others in my profession would disagree with me, I, personally, don't think I have the right *ever* to deliver that information in so many words. For one thing, I don't receive information as fact, written in black and white, or "spoken" in clear language. The DPs often communicate by "showing" me an object, pointing to a particular part of the body, or conveying a feeling, and it's always possible that I might be misinterpreting the signal they're sending. So, although it's certainly important—in fact, my duty and responsibility—to inform the living of anything their departed loved ones might want to tell them, there are ways to impart the information that allow me to be more comfortable and the sitter more receptive to what I have to say.

I might, for example, suggest that a DP has told me it's important for someone who's been estranged from his or her family to make amends. I might say that the DP advises a visit home, or asks that the person make contact with a certain aunt or uncle. My client will then be free to take the suggestion under advisement and act upon it, or not, as he or she wishes. And, in fact, as with everything else in life, we each have the free will to make that choice, and the choice we do make will affect the course of our own soul's journey, in this life and the next.

chapter four

the concept of
free choice

believe deeply in the existence of a Higher Power, and that belief has only been intensified in the course of my work. But as strongly as I believe in that Higher Power (whatever you, personally, choose to call it), I also *know* with equal conviction that He/She/It has given us the gift of free will, and where there is free will there must, by definition, be choice. That's why the DPs can't interfere with our ability to follow our own path, however much we might want them to make our decisions for us.

Think what the world, and your life on this plane, would be like without free will. There would never be any reason for you to make one choice rather than another—or, for that matter, to make any choices at all. What would be the meaning of terms like "morality," "ambition," or "motivation," or even good and evil? If everything in our lives—in this world and the next—were preordained, what would be the purpose of living? And how could we conceive of a Higher Power that was responsible not only for all the evil in the world but also for all our bad choices or bad actions? But, in fact, our souls' journeys are not preordained. They are determined by the choices we make as the result of our gift of free will.

creating karma

Since karma is essentially an Eastern concept, many people in the West don't really understand it clearly. Often, when people talk about karma, they seem to think of it in terms of reward and punishment. When something bad happens to them, they assume they're being punished for something they did (and obviously think they shouldn't have done). But what *karma* really tells us is that all actions have consequences, and that we are responsible for the consequences of our actions. In Biblical terms, "as man soweth, so shall he reap," and from a scientific perspective, every action has a reaction. That's not the same thing as being *punished* for our bad actions.

In other words, if we, of our own free will, make a particular choice, that choice will have particular consequences. If we continue to make the same choices, they will continue to have the same consequences, and that's called staying on the *wheel of karma*. The wheel goes round and round—or, as the saying goes, what goes around comes around—and if we stay on it, we'll just keep traveling in circles. But, of course, we have a choice about that, too. We can choose to get off the wheel by making a different choice.

If we keep making the same choice, and each time we make that choice it has the same unhappy consequence, it's not because some Higher Power has preordained that we're never going to be happy. It's because we simply haven't yet learned from experience to make a different choice the next time. No one is punishing us; we're simply punishing ourselves. But, again, there's a reason for that.

karma and the soul's journey

To understand the full impact of the interaction between karma and free choice, you need to remember that your current life, or incarnation on this plane, is only one stop on the never-ending journey of your soul.

We've already talked about the fact that without free choice life would have no real purpose. We'd all just be sitting around waiting to find out what Someone Else had decided was going to happen to us.

But life does have a purpose; everything happens for a reason. And the reason you may not always be *aware* is that it may be the result of a choice made by your soul even before you arrived on this plane.

Because human perception on the physical plane is limited with relation to time and space, we are, for the most part, unaware of our soul's experience beyond this plane. William Wordsworth, the great romantic poet, put it most beautifully when he wrote, "our birth is but a sleep and a forgetting." But just because we're unaware in this life of the choices our soul might have made before we were "born," that doesn't mean we don't bring karma with us into this world. If we've been unable to get off the wheel and, consequently, have been traveling in circles, and if our soul has done all the work it can in the spiritual realm to move on to a higher plane, it may be that it requires a physical body to complete that work and take the next step in its journey. That is when "birth" as we know it occurs.

choosing your parents

The choices each one of us makes before we even arrive on this plane determine our physical identity and provide the basis or blueprint not only for this life but also for the Afterlife and the lives that are to come. None of us just "happens" to be here, and none of us just "happens" to be who we are. There's always a reason for our present identity, and that reason is the choice made by each individual soul before entering this plane about who his or her parents will be.

Those of you who've had a difficult or unhappy relationship with your parents, may not want to believe you could have made such a "bad" choice— you may even think I must be out of my mind to think you *could* have made such a choice. But I assure you, first of all, that I'm definitely not out of my mind, secondly, that there's no such thing as a "bad" choice, and third, that you definitely did choose your parents.

Why you chose the parents you did has to do with the particular lessons your soul needs to learn and the work it needs to do during this earthly phase of its journey. So, however it may appear to you, you've made a "good" choice for the growth of your soul. You need to be who you are, at this moment, during your present sojourn on this plane, and by choosing your parents, you've chosen, in effect, your own identity.

If your parents are loving and supportive, perhaps you need to learn to have more gratitude for the gifts you were given. If they're smothering and protective, perhaps that's because you needed to learn to be more assertive and independent. A child, whose parents die young, will have a particular kind of learning experience, while one who has to care for a mother or father in old age will have one that's very different. And in each of those situations, the lessons you learn are those you need to learn.

I don't know why any one particular soul makes his or her choice, and you may not know either—at least while you're still on this plane—but what I do know is that those choices are never arbitrary and "who" we are is never just a coincidence. There are reasons that may be beyond our human power to determine, but they are always made for a higher good, and for the spiritual elevation of the Soul.

choosing your family

When we choose our parents we are also—it should be obvious but often isn't—choosing an entire extended family. The dynamics that always play out within the context of that family also become part of the learning process.

Anyone who's had siblings knows how different one child can be from another, even when they're raised in the same household by the same parents. But the truth is that no two children are ever raised in *exactly* the same household. The eldest child, for example, came into the world as the first-born; his or her parents were probably relatively young and may not have had very much money. The mother may have stayed at home to care for her baby. Then let's say the youngest child is born several years later. That child has older siblings.

The family may, by now, be more financially secure, may even have moved from a city to the suburbs, and may live in a house rather than an apartment. Perhaps, by this time, the mother has gone back to work or is able to hire a nanny. The family that the youngest child is born into is very different from the one that welcomed the first.

As a result, these children will have very different experiences, even if there is no dramatic event or circumstance that sets one apart from the other. How they are treated will affect them for the rest of their lives. It becomes part of what each soul learns on its journey. And, of course, each of those children chose to be the eldest, the youngest, or somewhere in between. That, too, is the result of free will.

choosing your journey

Choosing your identity means much more than opting to be a cute, blonde cheerleader type rather than a plump, shy bookworm, although that's certainly basic to your identity. It also means that you've chosen the basic blueprint for your life, because who you are determines what experiences life will throw your way. It doesn't, however, mean that your entire life is preordained, and that you might as well just "go with the flow," so to speak, because nothing you can do will change what's already been determined. If that were true, it would negate the entire concept of free will and make your original choices pretty meaningless.

The fact is that you *do* have the power to affect what happens in your life. You may have chosen to be born into a family that's rich or poor, white or black, living in Beverly Hills or war-torn Africa, but how you *respond* to your experiences remains completely up to you. You might, for example, be a handsome, charismatic guy with loving and generous parents, who provide you with the best life has to offer, and you might blow it all by getting involved with drugs, committing a crime, and winding up in prison. That's a pretty extreme scenario, but not one that hasn't occurred. Or, you might be brought up by struggling parents in a third world country, excel in school, win a scholarship to Harvard, and become the doctor who's responsible for a revolutionary medical breakthrough. Once more an extreme, but not an impossible dream, especially if you consider the life of Nelson Mandela, who fought for the rights of his countrymen, was imprisoned for 30 years by the white ruling class, and emerged an even greater leader than when he went in.

I can't know, of course, what his specific program might have been, but I do know he chose the circumstances that would create his life, and that those years behind bars in South Africa were a necessary part of his journey. He could have reacted differently to his imprisonment; he could have come out bitter and broken, but he didn't. Instead his resolve, forged in adversity, became steelier than ever.

Once you've chosen your original set of circumstances, the trajectory of your life is determined by the responses you make—of your own free will—to those circumstances. The outcomes are not preordained; they are the results of your choices. Again, it all relates back to karma, and the fact that every choice we make will have particular consequences in our lives.

Life is a process, and everything that happens in our life becomes not only part of that process but also part of our soul's journey. To take an extreme but, unfortunately, not so unusual example, let's say that a child is abused or mistreated when he or she is very young. No two children will respond in exactly the same way to that treatment. One might become stronger, another might be toughened, a third could develop strong feelings of compassion and grow up to work in social services with abused children, while yet a fourth might become an abuser him- or herself.

There are always unlimited possibilities for how an individual will respond and what a soul will learn from the same set of circumstances. We as individuals may not realize to what extent our ongoing choices and the decisions we make as adults, are affected by those original choices, but the Soul knows, and we will find out—if not in this life, then in the next.

So we return once more to the question of why one person would make such apparently positive choices and another would seem to choose so badly. And, again, I must repeat that there are no bad choices. The choices you made originally—about who your parents would be and who, therefore, you yourself would become—were made because of the lessons your soul had to learn, and however you choose to respond to the consequences of those choices, you will be learning *something*, even if it's just that you need to learn to start making better choices.

the power of our vibrations

Each of us attracts particular people or circumstances into our lives, and the way we do that is through the vibrations we emanate. All life is composed of energy, whether it is on the physical plane or the spiritual energy of a soul that's left its physical body. That energy creates a vibratory power that attracts and connects with the energies of others.

I've already talked about the fact that it's tuning my vibrations to the same frequency as those given off by the DPs that allows me to receive their messages. So, it shouldn't be too difficult for you to understand that the vibrations you give off will be more or less in tune with the vibrations of other people, or simply other sources of energy.

Energy, as we know, never dies, and it's the continuing energy of love that connects us with those who have passed. But it's also energy that connects us to others on this plane. How many times have we heard someone say, after a blind date or after meeting a potential partner, "There just weren't any sparks between us." Or, "I liked him, but I simply wasn't attracted to him." It's the kind of vibratory energy that each of us emanates that determines who we will or won't be attracted to, and who we will or won't attract to ourselves.

We all know that someone who is cheerful, upbeat, and positive "signals" those qualities to the people around her, while someone who is depressed or who always looks at his glass as half empty signals those qualities as well. Our "outlook" is part of our reaction to the circumstances in our lives, and the signals we send will determine who or what we draw to us.

This is not to say, however, that depressed people will always attract other depressed people, or that those who are cheerful will necessarily draw only Pollyannas into their life. I'm sure you've heard the old cliché, "opposites attract," and sometimes that's true. But no matter who or what you attract, you may be sure it's for a reason, even if that reason isn't always apparent at the time.

Perhaps you've realized that you keep running into people who are needy in some way and demanding of your time and attention. "Why am I such a magnet for the wounded of the world," you may have asked yourself. Well, there might be any number of reasons, and I'm not pretending I know the answer—especially since I don't know *you*. But one reason in particular might be that your soul needs to learn patience or compassion in order to grow and move on. Another, equally valid reason, however, is that you might need to learn to say no. Or maybe you have a wonderful, close-knit group of friends who always seem to be there when you need them, offering their love and support. *Aren't I lucky*, you might think, *to know such generous people*. Well, need I say that "luck" had nothing to do with it? It's more likely that your soul just needed to learn to trust, to accept love, to look more positively on the world at large, or to learn more gratitude.

I see this kind of vibratory power at work all the time in my workshops and seminars. Invariably, people with similar experiences will be drawn together by the silent signals their energy gives off. For example, in one group session not so long ago, there were five people—all of whom had lost a son, a brother, or a cousin, all approximately the same age, all of them in a car accident—all sitting in the same row. That was not coincidence; it was the energy of the group experience asserting itself.

If you think about energy in terms of electricity, this may be easier to understand. There are two kinds of currents, AC and DC. Plugging in an appliance that works on AC current into a DC socket isn't going to make a connection and close the circuit (in fact, it will probably just blow a fuse). In human terms, the circumstances of our lives have created a certain kind of energy in us, which is reflected in the vibrations we give off, and those vibrations, in turn, attract people with similar vibrations into our lives. If we're emanating AC vibrations, we're not going to connect with people whose vibrations run on DC, and vice versa.

Here is an example of something that happened on a recent tour stop in Dallas, Texas:

I had been on tour for some weeks doing events and book signings to the point that when we arrived in Dallas, Texas, I decided for purposes of getting some rest, I would register in the hotel under an alias. I figured that at least this might divert some of the random calls when people know where I am staying, and thus provide me with a little breathing time. If you have ever done extensive travel, coupled with work, you will know what I am talking about. Just one day was all I was asking.

As it turned out, the hotel, in which the tour management had booked me, was having a Mary Kay convention, and it was also to be a tribute to the late founder, Mary Kay Ash. Dallas is the home base for the Mary Kay Company. This meant the hotel was fully booked and there were approximately 3,500 people attending the weeklong event. In addition to being under an alias, the hotel had graciously upgraded me to one of their premier suites with a separate living room, which I could use for the private séance that had been arranged while I was there instead of using the original room scheduled. They were making every effort to ensure my stay would be hassle free because of the convention. This turned out to be quite wonderful since the amount of people wandering around the hotel was tremendous, and the sitting had previously been scheduled in their

"Board Room" on the floor just above the Grand Ballroom. Not a chance for a quiet session there.

As the day arrived for the sitting, which was scheduled for 2 P.M., I was ready and centered in order to begin greeting the attendees by a half hour before the session was to begin. I fully expected some of the twelve people to already be knocking at the door of the suite in excited anticipation of what was to come. To my surprise, no one was arriving early as usually happened. At first, I gave it some thought and decided with all the people downstairs at the Mary Kay event, it must be slowing down the participants' *arrival* or *getting* access to the elevators. Finally, it was 2 P.M., and still not a person had arrived. I began to wonder if I had mixed up the days in my mind and schedule. I am usually quite "on track" with things and have a wonderful assistant that supports me. One does tend, though, to drop into that syndrome of "what city am I in? Or, what day is it?" when you are traveling extensively. So, I waited.

By 2:10 P.M., I was really certain that something was amiss and put in a call to my assistant, Linda, in New York. There was no answer and I could only leave a message. Not much comfort for someone that by now was moving into anxiousness. I then called the Front Desk to ask if anyone had asked for me? Not thinking, I had only asked the desk clerk if anyone had asked for Suzane Northrop. I had not stated my suite number, which of course, was under the alias. Neither did I say I was Suzane Northrop. I tried once again to reach Linda to no avail. It was now 2:30 P.M. I could not figure this one out. I had checked my calendar and it confirmed this was the day. It was hard to believe that of twelve people, they would all not show up.

Suddenly, the phone in my suite rang. I rushed hurriedly to answer and it was a gentleman calling from the Concierge desk in the lobby of the hotel. "Ms. Northrop?" "Yes," I answered. "This is Dan at the Concierge desk, and I have a very upset group of about eight people here that I think are looking for you. Are you expecting them and may I send them up?" Relieved and excited, I said, "Yes, yes, please send them up right away."

It was almost 3 P.M. I opened the door to find eight people with perplexed and bewildered looks on their faces awaiting entrance. "Come in, come in, please," was my greeting. "What has happened and where have you been. I have been worried." Now I will share the group's experience, which will serve to affirm my earlier statement that vibrations attract.

As the story unfolded, it was revealed that each person had arrived at least 20 to 30

everything happens for a reason

minutes before the session. Only two of the group had come together. Just as they were told, each had simply stepped to the Daily Events Board's posting for the day, and saw that the location was noted as the hotel's Board Room. They independently proceeded to the floor designated for their appointment. As they arrived, and mind you not all at the same time, they discovered nothing posted outside the room regarding Suzane Northrop, and the room had not been set for anything, so they returned to the lobby in search.

Independent of each other, they had either asked the Bell Captain or the Front Desk where the 'Suzane Northrop Event' was being held this afternoon. Of course, under Suzane Northrup, they only showed the evening event for another day altogether, and no registration showing me in the hotel. By this time, all were getting a bit upset and insistent to the staff that there was indeed something happening there today, and each committed to continuing the search. None of the group would give up. Now what is amazing is that in the midst of these 3,500 people in the hotel for the Mary Kay convention, one by one, the séance group were ultimately drawn back to the Daily Events Board at the same time for one last check. When the two that had come together spoke to the other about her frustration, the result was that each person approaching ended up connecting to the others as the conversation was overheard and became magnified.

Ultimately, they unanimously decided to make one last try and all ended up at the Concierge's desk. Dan happened to be one of the few people working that day who knew of my alias, as well as my suite number. (I had some media interviews to do and the instruction for them had been to check in at the Concierge desk.) On top of it all, the hotel had failed to notify my assistant, Linda, of the room change, so she wouldn't have realized the "glitch" even if I had gotten through to her.

After hearing this story, we all had a good laugh and were able to engage in the séance as planned. It was clear that like vibrations of their intent for coming that day was part of the drawing together of this group of people that ultimately turned into a group quest. Not much to anyone's surprise, we would discover other connections as we engaged in the focus of the afternoon. No coincidences here. What is the possibility that any others would have given up and left?

Whatever people or circumstances come into your life, you need to understand that they're there because you attracted them, through your vibrations, and that there's always a reason. You also need to understand that if you're suffering, it's your doing. You're punishing yourself. God, or the Higher Power, does not take revenge upon you for past transgressions by punishing you in this life. That's not, as I hope I've already made clear, what this life is all about. On the contrary, God loves you and will do everything in His or Her power to help you learn and make better choices for yourself. But, again, whether or not you choose to do that is up to you.

making positive changes

By now it may sound as if I'm telling you that once your soul has made that initial choice as to who your parents and your family are going to be, you're more or less left on your own to "sink or swim," depending on how smart or how slow you are about making choices. But that's not true, either. It's always possible to change the trajectory of your life for the better (or for the worse, if you choose that route) by changing the vibrations you give off and, therefore, attracting a different kind of energy. It's all about choice. And those on the spiritual plane are there to help you do that in whatever way they can. One of the most positive ways they have of helping is by letting you know that they're present, well, and happy, and that they're still connected to you so that you will be better able to let go of the past and move on. Another is to put a particular person or circumstance in your path. That's to help you work out any karmic issues you may need to resolve. It's never about punishment. It's about providing opportunities for each soul in its never-ending path of learning and growth.

Depending on the course our life has taken—and remember that there are always reasons for that course in direct relation to each soul's program—we may be struggling with unresolved issues from our past that are preventing us from making better choices and moving on with our life in the present and future. We usually know when that's happening but we don't always know why. We may wonder why we keep making the same mistakes over and over again. We may wonder why we aren't happier. In earlier times, we might have said we were "sick at heart." Or our physical health might be suffering. Modern proponents of alternative medicine may think they've discovered the "mind/body connection," but the ancient Indian philosophy, upon which Ayurvedic medicine is based, has for centuries understood the intimate correlation between emotional and physical health. When we become aware of any of these disturbances in our life, what we're really feeling, although we don't normally put it in so many words, is that our soul is out of balance and we need to find a way to put it right.

One woman, who came to see me following the death of her brother, had also lost both her parents years before, when she was very young. As an adult, she kept meeting men who simply couldn't commit to a long-term relationship. She knew that this had become a pattern in her life, but she didn't understand that she was attracting those men *because* of their inability to commit, and she was at a loss to know how to break the pattern.

People who are struggling with abandonment issues react in different ways. Sometimes they sabotage their relationships by constantly asking their partner to "prove" over and over again that he or she really loves them and isn't going to leave. People who do that are likely to attract partners who don't mind being "put on trial" and who need to prove their loyalty as much as their partner needs to have it proved. Or, like the woman in this story, they emanate abandonment vibrations that continue to attract people who will fulfill their unconscious expectations. I explained to her that she needed to identify the patterns in her own life that were causing her to repeat the same experience over and over— like Sisyphus endlessly rolling that proverbial rock up the hill. By doing that, she'd be able to put her own soul back into balance and change the vibrations she was giving out, because we simply can't pull in anything that's outside our own vibrations.

I'm happy to say that she's finally met a man who, while still not willing to take the ultimate plunge into marriage, seems more willing than the others to change. They've moved in together, and my client has given this man a year to make the final commitment. By becoming aware of her own self-destructive vibratory pattern, she's been able to modify the signals her soul was sending out. By doing that, she's changing the trajectory of her journey.

Did my client's loved ones on the other side put this man in her path? I can't say for sure (because they haven't told me), but it's likely they did. They could *not,* however, make her decide to welcome him into her life. That was her choice. When it comes to making positive changes in your life, the DPs are always there to help. Because they love you, they want you not only to be happy but also to grow and evolve, and they'll do anything in their power to help put your soul on a positive path—and then they leave it up to you to make the choice.

Just how self-destructive we humans can be when our soul is out of balance, and how healing our contacts with those watching over (and out for) us can be, was dramatically manifested by a woman, I'll call Mary, whom I met on a recent retreat:

> Mary's mother had died of breast cancer when Mary was only twelve years old, which meant that she had grown up without the guidance and support of a female role model. The loss was so traumatic that she'd tried to take her own life on more than one occasion. And then, sadly, when she was in her thirties, Mary and her sister were also diagnosed with breast cancer. They both underwent radical mastectomies, and Mary also had a hysterectomy. At that point, this woman, who had been deprived of her mother's womanly guidance,

had now lost, given up, or destroyed virtually all of her own womanhood.

When I met her, she was also suffering from Carpel Tunnel Syndrome in both hands and was wearing what appeared to be leather gauntlets that fit over her hands and fore-arms. When she spoke, she unconsciously raised her gauntleted hands in front of her, as if to protect herself by preventing anyone from coming too close. She was in so much emotional pain she didn't realize that even with her body language she was trying to keep people away.

To me, it seemed clear that Mary was at a crossroads in her life. Either she'd have to find some way to come to terms with her mother's death and allow some love into her own life, or her life, too, would, effectively, be over. And because she understood this herself, she'd made the decision—of her own free will—to come to the retreat and try to change the direction of her journey.

During our session, Mary's mother came through immediately to let her daughter know she loved her and that she hadn't left her by choice, but that her death had been part of her own soul's journey and so a part of Mary's and her sister's as well. Although knowing this couldn't ever make up for hav-ing grown up and lived so long without a mother, the contact, as well as working with

a grief counselor, has brought Mary the closure she needed to resolve her pain so that,
hopefully, she'll be able to move beyond her
grief and change the destructive pattern in
which she'd been caught up.

the boundary program
and the gift of free will

If the trajectory of our soul's journey is determined
by the choices we make both before and during this
life, it shouldn't be hard to understand that, on the
one hand, free will does not end when we leave this
plane, or the other, and that our loved ones in spirit
cannot violate or deny our freedom of choice by
doing anything that would interfere with that journey.
They can, and will, do whatever is in their power to
help us on our way: by letting us know that they love
us no matter what their relationship with us might
have been here on earth; by helping us to move
beyond our grief or disappointment or anger; and by
putting particular people or circumstances in our path.
They cannot ignore the protocols of The Boundary
Program by giving us information we weren't meant
to have, either because it would somehow endanger
us or because it would prevent us from exercising the
choices we need to make for our own soul's edification
and elevation.

The DPs do get to make choices, and we have to
believe and learn to accept the fact that the choices

they make on our behalf are always for our own good. Whether or not the reason is immediately clear to us, they do have their reasons, and their reasons always have our best interests at heart. We may *think* we know what's best for us, but we can sometimes be wrong. In fact, every time we make a choice, we must *think* at the time that it's the right choice— none of us, after all, would purposely go about making self-defeating choices—but how often do we find out later that it's just what we have done?

That's why I always emphasize to my clients that they shouldn't necessarily expect to get the message they think they'd *like* to receive. Our loved ones aren't holding out on us just to annoy us or make us unhappy. They love us and don't want us to be unhappy, but they know—as we may not—that telling us what we think we want to hear won't always be to our benefit in the long run. That does very little to support our growth.

Although we, on the physical plane, are limited in our perspective by constraints of time and space, the DPs are not. Our knowledge is limited by the bounds of our awareness. The DPs, on the other hand, may be beyond time and space, but they are bound not to interfere with the learning process through which, by responding to the circumstances of our life, we expand our own awareness and so enhance our spiritual growth.

But it's also up to us to pay heed to the messages we *do* get. The phone lines between the physical and spiritual planes are open on both ends, and we have the free choice of listening or not listening to what's coming through.

redirecting and preventing negative energy

The more we become aware of the unresolved issues that may be creating negative energy and preventing us from making good choices, the better able we'll be to redirect that energy and create more positive vibrations that will pull in people or circumstances that can enhance the quality of our lives. Just as our choices can make our own lives better or worse, so can they affect the lives of others. But if we make poor choices or perform evil deeds that bring pain and suffering, not only to ourselves but also to those around us, it's never because some power beyond our control *made* us do it.

I would like to share with you some situations where clearly the choices had a major impact on other people's lives. In all these cases, they could have chosen to go in a different direction with their choice.

1. Look at Shirley MacLaine. The choice she made ultimately guiding her to bring her experiences and thoughts to paper have influenced so many people's lives around the subject of the spirit realm and beyond. Certainly there has been an enormous

amount of negative talk about her. Yet, her choice has resulted in quite an impact on so many lives, in a positive way, opening them up to new ways of thinking about the *spiritual journey*. Her choice was literally to go *out on a limb* to help others. (Sorry, I couldn't resist that.)

2. There was a woman in Idaho, who had five sons, and lost five sons. All five were hemophiliacs and as the result of transfusions over the years, all contracted AIDS. One by one she lost her sons. Because of the stigma of AIDS in her city, most people turned their back on her and offered no support. She was _desperate for some kind of emotional help, and as she continued to explore the community, found none. This would have been difficult for anyone to bear without turning anger toward a city she had lived in all her life. It happened that one of her sons was gay. And, even though she knew very little about her son's lifestyle, she ultimately turned to the gay community. To her amazement, she found that within this community there were many with the AIDS virus, or full-blown AIDS that had chosen to remain silent for fear of rejection. They had no one either. What resulted in this

connection was that this woman created a home for those in need to provide support emotionally, medically, and nurtured the body and spirit. Not only did this orchestrate a service that was worthwhile, it also created a whole new family of sons for her in which she was surrounded by enormous support and love.

3. There have been many occasions in my seminars, lectures, and séances where I have had a parent attend wanting to make contact with their *favorite child* who has passed over. Now, when we say *favorite child* that to me indicates that there are more children and that they are somehow *not* the favorites. What I have seen time and again is that the grieving of this child that had special meaning quite often ends up in neglect of the children still present. I have even had the DPs of those children come through with messages that have asked the parent what they were doing about the child remaining. How do you suppose this affects the child living? In one case I know of, the child that was alive ultimately shot himself (and he was a twin) because he could not bear the process of grieving his brother alone. He felt he didn't matter and that no one was there for

him. Fortunately, he survived and is well
on the road to physical and emotional
recovery *with* his parents at his side.

4. Look at Eric Clapton and what resulted
   from his son's fall to death out of a high
   story building. His despair and anger
   could have resulted in him closing off
   and hiding his intense feelings, but he
   wrote *Tears in Heaven*, and shared it
   with the world. This gave us all an
   opportunity to look at love, grief, and
   healing. To my thinking, this also gave
   every parent in the world that has lost
   a child something to identify with that
   gave a sense of understanding and
   connection.

5. I am also reminded of what using anger
   in a positive way can create when I
   think what choices the mother(s) had
   that created MADD (Mothers Against
   Drunk Driving) out of a senseless death
   by a drunk driver. I had a woman in a
   seminar that told how years before she
   had been constantly obsessed with the
   "notion" that her son would be killed
   by a drunk driver. She would make him
   promise that he would not get in the car
   with someone who had been drinking
   when he was out with friends. He had

always been a great son and a popular student. As her story progressed, she shared that once again she had warned her son about riding with drinking drivers as he readied to pick up friends for a high school graduation party. He assured her he wouldn't. At the end of the night as he returned home, he was unable to park in his usual place in front of his house, and parked directly across the street. As he got out and started across toward the house, he was hit by a car and killed. The driver was drunk. This story came out as I spoke about the choice of the mother that created MADD, and the woman speaking said she was grateful there had been somewhere to go after her son's death for support. Another choice made in the positive direction.

The examples above are obviously about people who have made a choice for positive results, and then we have Osama bin Laden and the events of September 11, or anyone else in history that has abused their power. Just think about what that kind of power and finances could have done if it had been directed for the good of the world. I think you get what I am trying to say here.

There's no Higher Power that can *make* us do anything we don't choose to do. We create our own negative energy. We can also choose to create positive energy as well. And until, through our own free will, we do make the choices that will change or reverse that energy, we'll continue to emanate those negative vibrations.

But we *can* change—we can always change, although it may not always be in a single lifetime. Depending how powerful that negative energy has been, or how destructive our actions—either to ourselves or to others—it may take several lifetimes to completely reverse and rebalance the trajectory of our soul. This is the way of karma.

What we all must constantly try to remember is that positive growth and change are *always* possible, and that it's absolutely within our power to reverse, moderate, or remediate the course of our journey.

the gift of grace

If you're now examining your life and thinking that you must have made a lot of poor choices to build up so much negative karma to work through, I want to assure you that even though your choices are your own, God or the Higher Power is always there to step in and help.

If you're doing all you can to change your negative energy, to get off the wheel of karma, and to grow, God will notice that. And because God is a loving God, your mistakes are immediately forgiven so that you won't have to continue carrying that negative karma or guilt when you go into spirit or into another lifetime. Besides, mistakes only serve as a greater opportunity for learning how to better move into the right action or the right direction. I quite like the quote of Miles Davis that says, "Do not fear mistakes—there are none," to which I'll add, as long as we look for the lesson—the *gift* that lies within that miscalculation.

That is the gift of Grace.

chapter five

every soul
has a program

the Soul Program lies at the heart of our reason for being. It provides the blueprint or map of our journey, the circumstances that will create our reactions, and teach—or not teach—us the lessons we need to learn. There are certain things that are preset by each soul before birth, and there are some that are set as you are born, like time, birth sign, etc. As for any soul, there are certain things you learn through the human existence that are the only way you can learn about "those" things. There is something that happens during the human experience that can happen on no other level. The good news is that we really can handle most of it. Our experience here is all about what we do with what we are presented. There are certain programs that take lifetimes to complete. Take Mozart for example. He had to be working on his own specific Soul Program to be able to compose as he did at five-years-old. Something had certainly been evolving in his journey. It clearly wouldn't have worked for him to have Einstein's program that would have gotten in the way of the music he was to create as Mozart. Think of The Soul Program as the sturdy trunk of a tree with many branches feeding into and off of its roots. Two of the thickest and strongest of those branches are The Boundary Program and the Gift of Free Will.

the soul program and free choice

In fact, our program begins with our initial choice. How you choose to come into this world determines the basic blueprint of your journey. Let's say, for example, that one of your parents dies very young, or when you are very young. You need to remember that you chose that parent for a reason, whether or not you're aware what the reason might be. And your parent also chose to come into this world as someone who wouldn't live a long life. You are each part of the other's program because you each had something to teach the other.

Perhaps the reasoning of choice for your parent was that he or she needed to learn how to let go and move on because they had been unable to do that in a previous life. And perhaps you needed to learn how to cope with loss. Any lesson left unlearned in one life will have to be learned in the next—either here on earth or in the spiritual realm. If a person hasn't learned to deal with loss in one lifetime, they will have to come back and experience loss again in another. Then if he or she simply doesn't learn to move through loss and the circumstances in his life in a positive way, they will have to continue that lesson until it is learned.

If all this sounds too much like being left back in school, I assure you that The Soul Program has nothing to do with punishment. It does, however, have everything to do with karma. Your free will is a gift, but with that gift also comes an obligation— the obligation to use your gift of free will constructively, because if you squander your *gifts*, you might lose them.

There are, in fact, two kinds of karma. There is the karma created by the gifts we've gained and what we do with them, but there is also the karma that results from the debts we owe. As we balance out or repay our debts, being conscious along the way not to create any new ones, we'll be able to move to the next stage of our journey. We will have completed some aspect of our Soul Program. But if, on the other hand, our reactions create new debts, we'll have to balance those as well. Nevertheless, it's all part of the learning experience. The thing to remember is that karma is only changeable through some sort of intervention on our part.

There is a blueprint for each of our lives that's created at the moment our soul makes its original choice, but not everything that happens to us after that is either preordained or necessary. That's where "consciousness" comes in. The route of our journey is altered by the conscious choices we make along the road. And although two people may have very similar experiences and may even appear to be taking the same route, no two people will ever react in exactly the same way with the same energy to whatever it is they encounter on life's highway. Therefore, no two people will ever have exactly the same program or the same experience. I encourage you on this planetary journey as a human being to stay alert to the road signs of life in a metaphorical sense: Caution, No U-Turns, Yield, Stop, Steep Incline, No Passing, and Dead End. We all get those signals from within, as well as, traveling down the literal highway as part of a support system on our journey.

vibratory synchronicity and karmic patterns

Since everything happens for a reason—although not everything that happens is necessary—there are always reasons why we appear to be attracting particular people, or particular kinds of people, into our lives. There are Soul Groups and Soul Patterns that certainly are centered around working on specific issues. You can be part of a Soul Group that has committed to work on issues with your own soul. And there are Soul Patterns that can be supported by other souls outside your Soul Group to also help your own soul work through certain issues. Each has its own vibration and will draw to it, like a magnet, those here on Earth to assist in that specific learning process. They come "into" our life path not by coincidence but by a higher plan with an intended reason.

The first reason is certainly our vibratory synchronicity—the fact that we are emanating similar vibrations because of our similar emotional energy. Remember the group at the hotel in Dallas. I've already mentioned that I frequently see this happening in seminars and workshops when people who have suffered similar losses seem "coincidentally" to find themselves seated close to one another when they could have chosen to sit anywhere at all in a fairly large room.

What causes that vibratory synchronicity is the fact that these people have similar karmic patterns or that they've shared similar experiences. But karma also works in another way when it comes to the people we seem to "run into" again and again. Those people show up either because they need to teach us something or because we have something to teach them— probably both. It's not necessarily the specific *person* that we draw into our lives, but the *lesson* we can learn from or teach him or her. Karma, as I've said, is about cause and effect, actions creating reactions, and how we react to one another determines whether we'll get off or stay on the *wheel* of negative karmic patterning. If one person has a need and another person has the solution to that need, those two people will surely be drawn together. And so, if there's a person in your life who seems to be sticking like a painful thorn in your side no matter how hard you've tried to pry yourself loose or shake yourself free, what you've got to understand is that that person is there for a reason, to teach you something—even though the lesson may be a painful one.

Those vibrations also bring others with similar experiences together so you may support each other in the process of healing and moving on. I remember one such seminar where in the same section, I had seven people that ended up sitting next to each other who had lost a male between the ages of 17 to 19 by freak accidents. This more times than not is a frequent situation I encounter. These people have the opportunity to share and identify with others of like circumstances in order to begin the healing process.

Psychologists have determined that very often abusive people come from abusive homes and have been abused themselves, while those they abuse are likely to move from one abusive situation to the next. Both these behaviors are related to karma and The Soul Program. Both the abusers and their victims will continue to follow those patterns until they are able to make different choices and get off the wheel. So, if you're an abuser, don't blame your behavior on your parents, and if you continually find yourself in abusive situations, don't blame your abusers because, in either case, you're the ones who are creating the pattern. As I've said, it's also possible for someone who was abused as a child to make different choices, to develop compassion and caring for others who've experienced what he or she went through. No one's response to any situation or treatment is "written in stone."

That said, however, I've also seen patterns of suicide and mental illness passed down through families. When people choose to be born into such a family—when they choose, in effect, to stay on the wheel—they're choosing the abuse, the suicide, or the mental illness, but also the stigma, the guilt, the blame, and all the other emotional baggage that goes along with being part of that kind of pattern. Why people make those choices I can't say, because the reason is probably different for each one of them, and the lessons they take away from the same situation will also be different.

A good friend of mine, who throughout her life had been tagged "unlucky in love," finally met a wonderful man. He was a successful stockbroker, divorced with two children, who'd always lived life on a roller-coaster of emotional highs and lows. He and my friend fell in love and decided to live together even though they chose not to get married. They both were happier than they'd ever been in their lives until, one day, this man who was now more content than ever before in his life, jumped out the window of their apartment while my friend was in the next room. Why did he do that? Perhaps he just wanted to go out when he was on an emotional high. Perhaps he couldn't cope with being in a relationship. I don't know. But my friend, who was devastated, was also completely shut out by his family, who blamed her for his suicide, from any participation in the funeral and was prevented from any public mourning. Why these two people needed to find one another will probably remain a mystery even to me, but their programs brought them together for a reason, to learn from one another, and his manner of death was his choice alone. My friend not only didn't cause it; she was not to blame for the choice that he made.

In this context, you might also remember the woman in a Chapter 4 who kept attracting men who were unwilling to commit. It was she who made those choices because she hadn't yet learned to deal with the abandonment issues that were the legacy of her parents' early deaths. Out of love, her DPs were helping her to learn to make better choices by putting a different kind of man in her path, but it would still be up to her to decide how she would choose to react to this new relationship and the opportunity that was created for her. Which brings us to the relationship between The Boundary Program and The Soul Program.

there are boundaries the DPs can't cross

We've already discussed the fact that the DPs can't enter your vibration without being invited and that they won't provide you with any information they know will put you in harm's way, but, most important of all, they can't do anything that would interfere with your greatest gift—the gift of free choice.

In her final book, *The Afterlife Codes*, the medium Susy Smith writes about a message she received from her mother, who was also her guardian angel. Guardian angels, her mother told her, "can give suggestions and warnings that may be extremely helpful to us on occasion, but they do not want to tell us what to do with our lives, for it is by making our own decisions that we grow."

In a nutshell, that message explains everything The Soul Program is about. Because they love us, our DPs want what is best for us, and what is best for us is achieving spiritual growth. They'll help in any way they can, but it wouldn't be helpful for them to interfere with the decision-making that is necessary for us to achieve that spiritual development.

Here are two instances where DPs delivered messages to loved ones on this plane that allowed them to change the course of their journey—if they chose to do so:

A woman called in when I was doing a radio program, explaining that she'd spoken to me before, shortly after her father had passed. Now her mother, too, had died and this woman was hoping to make contact with her as well. I picked up immediately that her mother was there, but for some reason she seemed to be rather crabby, just generally not in a very good mood. When I told this to the caller, she explained that her mother had lost her entire family in the Holocaust and, because of that, had found it very difficult to express love to her own daughter.

The daughter then told me that when I'd contacted her father, he'd suggested that she go home and "give your mother a kiss from your dad." Even though her relationship with her mother had always been strained, she was determined to listen to what her father had to say. She didn't know why, but she felt it must be the right thing to do, so she went home and made a point of giving a kiss to her mother. The mother then passed suddenly a few days later.

Imagine how different the rest of this woman's life would have been if she'd neglected to take her father's advice and her mother had passed without her having taken the opportunity to deliver this loving message. She could have made that other choice, and she'd have learned a lesson that way, too.

On another, more recent occasion, I was doing a reading for a young man whose father had been in the military. Since his death, his family had become estranged, and the children were no longer talking to one another. I'm not sure what the problem was, but the DP let his son know that this was not what he would have wished for his family. He didn't want his sons to be in conflict with one another.

The young man told me afterwards, that he'd let his brothers know what his father had said. He wasn't certain that they'd be able to reconcile their differences, but at least he'd done what he could to carry out his father's wishes. It was, nevertheless, his choice. His father couldn't make any of his children do what he wanted (maybe, as a military man, he did that in life), but he could give the one who was willing an opportunity to change not only the path of his own life, but that of his brothers as well.

I should also add, however, that there are many times when the DPs are trying to tell us something and we're just too preoccupied with our own preconceived notions of what we think we ought to be hearing to listen properly. Time and again people come to me for readings with their minds already set on the one message they're sure will prove my legitimacy. If they don't hear exactly what they think they should, they either discount the connection entirely or they insist on questioning me and twisting my words desperately trying to get me to say it exactly the way they want to hear it. Nothing else will do.

If you've already decided what your DP will say, you'll never be able to hear anything else—you're creating a kind of self-imposed deafness. And why people would do that continues to astound me. It would suggest to me that you really aren't interested—or maybe you are afraid—to hear what the DPs want to say, therefore, you decide what is to be said and how. Not much open-mindedness operating here. We do it with our living loved ones as well when we insist that they tell us they love us in exactly the words we want to hear, and we assume if they *don't* say it that way then it's obvious they really don't love us. But that's not any truer of the living than it is of the dead. Some people unfortunately want to stay in their pain. It has a certain payoff for them somehow. They build an attachment to either the outcome or the attention it may bring—be it positive or negative.

learning to read
your own blueprint

At this point, I suspect many of you may be wondering how you can determine what your own program is and whether or not you're making good choices for yourself around "getting" the lessons you are to be learning. A friend of mine once told someone, when asked how to find the next thing they should be working on, to look at what in your life right now is annoying or irritating to you, and you will have it. Sometimes the very thing we are looking for is right under our nose. We are certainly guided intuitively toward the right choice. We are very clever sometimes when it comes to diverting ourselves "off course." When that happens, it is usually the *ego mind* working out of some fear.

If you are really sincere about finding your program, one good way to start would be to just sit down with a pencil and paper and start to make a list: Do you have one living parent or two? Do you have siblings? Are you adopted? What is your ethnic background? Is your family religious? Rich or poor? All these variables set up patterns in your life. Once you've made your list, try to determine what problems, issues, or conflicts in your life—usually recognizable as patterns—seem to be connected to these particular circumstances and what lessons you might have learned or need to learn as a result.

If, for example, you're a strong, independent person whose family was very controlling and tried

137

to strip you of your independent identity, why would you have chosen such a family? Perhaps it was to challenge you on just that point, to make you work harder to develop your personality and to become even stronger. I see this dynamic quite often playing out with people that have names with a Jr., the II, or the III after their names.

Whenever I do a workshop or seminar, I always ask people at the beginning why it is they think they're there, what aspect of their journey they think they need to work on.

I think that all of us "know" on some level when our lives are going badly, when something just seems to be "out of whack," when something destructive is consuming us, or when we continue to find ourselves in an endless cycle of destructive situations or relationships over and over again. When you see that you're repeating a nonproductive pattern, it's usually because you're operating outside your own vibratory pattern.

Now, if you've done what I've suggested and made a list, and if you still can't figure out why you seem to be making such poor choices, there are other ways to get help. You might have your astrological or numerological chart done by a legitimate astrologist or numerologist, if that's in keeping with your own belief system. Knowing how your stars or numbers line up can help you to see where you've "gone off the chart." Or you might enter traditional therapy with a qualified professional who can help you recognize aspects of yourself that you might not be able to see on your own. If you've suffered a loss, joining a support group for people who are struggling with issues or problems similar to your own can also be extremely helpful. These days there is also quite a number of professionals specializing in grief therapy. A group called *Compassionate Friends*, for example, brings together people who are coping with the loss of a child. There are also groups for suicide survivors and for those whose loved ones are dying of a terminal illness, or have died of diseases like cancer or AIDS.

And sometimes communicating with the DPs will clarify the pattern as nothing else can. Here's what happened when a woman came to me for a private reading because she wanted to contact her sister:

> Marjorie's sister had always had a deathly fear of flying, but because she owned an import/export business that required her traveling to Europe, she had to fly fairly frequently. Even so, she never quite managed to overcome her fear, and before one particular trip to Paris she confessed to Marjorie that the fear was greater than ever.
>
> Marjorie tried to reassure her sister by telling her that she was probably just anxious about other things and by reminding her that she'd always been afraid and nothing had ever happened to her in all the years she'd been flying. "But," Marjorie said to her, "if you're so afraid, why not make sure you book your flight on Swissair, which has never

had a single fatality in its entire history. That way you can be certain you'll be safe." The fearful sister followed Marjorie's advice and booked herself on the Swissair Flight 800 that crashed into the Atlantic Ocean off the coast of Long Island, killing all on board.

My client was left not only to mourn the death of her sibling and closest friend but also to deal with the terrible guilt she felt for having been the one to suggest that her sister book that flight in the first place. She just couldn't get over the knowledge that she'd been the cause of Marjorie's changing her plans, and that if she hadn't done that, she'd still be alive.

When her sister came through during our session, however, she assured Marjorie that she had nothing to feel guilty about. Now that she'd passed, she let her sister know, she understood that her lifelong fear of flying had grown out of the fact that her soul had known all along it would be her fate to die in a plane crash—it was part of her program and had nothing at all to do with any advice Marjorie might or might not have given her.

By making this contact, Marjorie learned not only that it was her sister's program to pass as she did, but also that her own program had determined that she would be a "survivor," and that at least one of the lessons written into her blueprint meant that she'd have to learn how to deal with that aspect of her journey in a positive way. Notice that Marjorie's sister didn't actually tell her that part of it, but by explaining what had been in her own program, she also provided the information that *allowed* Marjorie to become aware of the original choice she had made (to come into the world as the sister of this particular person), and of the choices she would have to make in the future.

death can be a wake-up call

Whatever it was that brought Marjorie to me— and surely the reasons were at least in part her love for her sister and her need to be absolved of her guilt—the message she received was both comforting and enlightening. But sometimes just experiencing the death of a loved one can, in and of itself, help to clarify your own program.

Once death has touched you personally, you never look at it the same way again. When someone close to you dies, it can change your entire belief system and clarify your program in a dramatic way.

If you've ever read what people have said about their Near Death Experiences, you'll probably have noticed that in almost every instance they viewed death differently after the experience than they had before. Having gone on that journey, they understood that "death" is a transition rather than a conclusion, they lost their fear, and they saw "life" differently as well.

But you don't have to have your own Near Death Experience to achieve this kind of enlightenment. The death of someone dear to you can sometimes provide the same kind of "awakening." Even if you haven't been aware of your own program before, the very fact that your child, your spouse, or even a close friend has died will provide you with the basic information that this particular kind of loss is part of your program. And if you're already aware of the fact that you *do* have a program, you can begin to think about what in particular it is you're supposed to be learning from the experience. Experiencing a death, in other words, can be "enlightening" in a very profound and life-changing way.

If we've experienced too much loss in our lives, that can set up a pattern as well. We may think we simply can't bear to lose anyone else, and so, in self-defense, we begin to push away those who are closest to us. That's what happened to a friend of mine when she experienced multiple deaths in a very short time. She started to withdraw emotionally from her husband. She just didn't want to be comforted because she feared what might happen if that comforting person was somehow lost to her as well. He was trying to be loving and supportive and she just kept pushing him away. His feelings were understandably hurt, and their relationship was becoming more and more strained, until she finally recognized the fact that by rejecting the one person who loved her the most, she was only creating more loss for herself.

If, like my friend, we are able to look at ourselves clearly and gain that kind of insight, experiencing a death can be an opportunity for self-examination, a chance for us to take another look at the negative or positive patterns we may have been creating for ourselves, and a chance to get off the wheel of karma and turn those patterns around.

it's always part of the program

After the tragedy at the World Trade Center on September 11, 2001, many people asked me whether a disaster of that magnitude could have occurred outside the program of those who died. Was it possible, they wondered, that all those people could have been meant to die in that terrible way, or could it have been merely an accident or their bad luck to be in those buildings at that time.

My answer is always the same: I don't believe in "accidents" and there's no such thing as bad luck or coincidence any more than what happens to us is ever a punishment. Difficult as it may be to accept, if those people were supposed to be there, either in those buildings or on those planes, it was just part of their program.

In the news reports following the crash of Flight 93, David Beamer, the father of Todd Beamer, who was one of the leaders of the passengers' efforts to overcome their hijackers, was quoted as saying, "I've, of course, asked myself many times why our beautiful son was on that plane. We know why he was on it. The faces of evil—those particular hijackers—they got on the wrong plane." If he hadn't known before, certainly after that crash, Mr. Beamer appears to have understood that the manner of his son's death was part of his program and that his being on that plane was no accident or unfortunate coincidence.

In fact, Todd would normally have left for his Tuesday business meeting in California on Monday evening, but he and his wife, Lisa, had just returned from a five-day trip to Italy. Lisa was pregnant with their third child, and he was anxious to spend some time with his two young sons, so he decided to take the early-morning plane on Tuesday instead. Was he reluctant to leave because he had some premonition of what was to come? I can't know that, but I do know there was a very good reason for his not leaving at his usual time.

And, then there was a touching interview with Lisa Beamer, Todd's wife, on the TV show *Good Morning America*. She shared that what had come for her was she realized it was the little things she missed most about Todd—such as hearing the garage door open as he came home, and her children running to meet him. She's now the mom of another beautiful little girl since his death.

I will paraphrase the story Lisa recalled on the show that morning and has recently surfaced on the Internet:

Lisa told about this special teacher she'd had many years ago in high school whose husband died suddenly of a heart attack. About a week after his passing, she decided rather than not say anything about it to her students that she would share some of the insights she'd come to understand. Just before it was time for class to be over on that particular summer afternoon, she moved a few things aside on the edge of her desk and sat down.

She paused, looked at the class, and with a gentle look of reflection on her face she said, "Class is over. I would like to share with all of you, a thought that is unrelated to class, but which I feel is very important. Each of us is put here on earth to learn, share, love, appreciate, and give of ourselves. None of us knows when this fantastic experience will end. It can be taken away at any moment. And, when something is taken away suddenly, perhaps it is God's way of telling us that we must make the most out of every single day."

As her eyes began to water, Lisa told the audience, the teacher went on to say, "So, I would like you all to make me a promise. From now on, on your way to school, or on your way home, find something beautiful to notice. It doesn't have to be something you see, it could be a scent, perhaps of freshly baked bread wafting out of someone's house, or it could be the sound of the breeze slightly rustling the leaves in the trees, or the way the morning light catches one autumn leaf as it falls gently to the ground. Please look for these things, and cherish them. For, although it may sound trite to some, these things are the 'stuff' of life: the little things we are put here on earth to enjoy, the things we often take for granted. We must make it important to notice them, for at anytime it can all be taken away."

Lisa said the class was completely quiet. She said they all picked up their books and filed out of the classroom silently. Then Lisa said that on her way home from school that afternoon, she noticed more things than she had in that whole semester.

At the close of the interview, Lisa said that remembering that time back in high school, with the recent death of Todd and so many others, she now tries daily to appreciate all of those things that we so often overlook. She said she remembers what an impression that teacher made on her because the remembrance was as strong today as it was for her on that *day*.

Lisa was a great reminder to all of us that no one knows if he or she or anyone in his or her life will be here in the next five minutes. Don't hold back on expressing yourself. Tell that special person today how you feel, give a hug, cast a smile instead of a frown, and don't forget to tell those you love that you love them. I know because I live in New York City. After that day of tragedy, I saw New Yorkers speaking to each other in a different way—and visitors, too. Now, I see smiles, laughter, and tears shared openly. I see people opening doors for another person, and have watched the pace down the sidewalks become a bit slower. It's always been a beautiful city with beautiful people to me, and now we are showing it to everyone.

So as Lisa suggested, so do I—slow down, take notice of something special you see on your lunchtime today—and if you haven't stopped to take lunchtime in a while because you are *too busy*, then do so. Go barefoot. Or walk on the beach or through the park at sunset. Stop off on the way home tonight to get a double dip ice cream cone or have a chat with your neighbor. For as we continue through our lives, it is not the things we did that we often regret, but the things we didn't do. Don't let one thing, one moment go by unnoticed because that is part of The Soul Program too.

I know this may sound harsh, but every death is a tragedy to someone, and the World Trade Center tragedy, while it was of a far greater magnitude, was truly not different in kind from the tragedies experienced by individuals every day. The hijackers deaths were also tragedies to their loved ones, and their actions were also part of their programs. Speculation about the reasons for their having committed such acts places blame both on the poverty of their lives and on the charismatic influence of their leader. But again, it all comes back to karma. The circumstances of their lives put them in the position of making choices, and they made the choices they did of their own free will. One can only imagine what lessons their souls were meant to learn, but I know absolutely that they were in those planes for a reason, just as surely as were their captives.

and what about evil?

I don't believe I'm in a position to pass judgment on the actions of those hijackers—or on anyone's actions for that matter—and I've already said that The Soul Program is not about reward and punishment. But the fact remains that there is evil in the world, and that committing evil deeds is also a choice. I believe that if we choose to do evil, our "punishment," if that's what you choose to call it, is that we no longer have the privilege to reincarnate as an individual. But I also believe that giving up that privilege is, in and of itself, a choice, because we chose to commit that evil deed in the first place. By relinquishing that privilege, we return to the *Oversoul* or *Soul Patch* and become part of the undying cycle of energy, but we are deprived of the opportunity for further individual evolution. I do believe that this Soul Patch is like setting our soul into a recycling pattern. To me, this is what the Bible means when it talks of Hell. I have visions of Robin Williams entering the zone of lost souls in the movie, *What Dreams May Come*. It's as if the soul in this case can't move forward and it can't move back. It is "stuck" in the same scene for all time. This is where I would imagine a soul like Hitler's resides. The evil he manifested caused him the loss and privilege of reincarnation.

can the soul ever know in advance?

Your soul knows much more than your conscious mind can ever be aware of. When we leave this plane and return to the Oversoul we also retain our individual soul, (unless, as I've said, we relinquish that privilege by choosing to relinquish the gift of free choice) and our individual soul consciousness, which means that we retain all our learning from past lives and this life. It all goes into either a soul or personality bank, and when we reincarnate, we bring that learning with us. The cache of ageless learning can give us the ability in any certain "earth life" to do extraordinary things. Remember Mozart? If, for example, we've been learning to become stronger and more self-assertive, we might choose parents who were very controlling. Their personality might make our life more difficult, and we might have no conscious understanding of why that is, but we'd be learning to become even stronger. The choices we make are always the choices that will help us to grow, and although we, on this plane, might not understand why, our soul always knows and has made its choice for a reason. Some lessons may be painful or difficult, but if everything were easy, we'd never leave our comfort zone, and we'd never evolve.

Each soul's knowledge may extend even beyond that. In some instances, your soul might actually have a premonition or foreknowledge that it is about to leave this plane, although we might not consciously be aware of it. One woman, who came to a workshop I gave recently, had an experience that demonstrates how these premonitions can occur. I'll call her Janiece.

> Janiece had been in a long-term relationship with a married man, and while she was out of town on one particular occasion she received numerous phone calls from him. She traveled a lot for her work and this was not his usual modus operandi, but she really didn't think very much of it and just assumed that he was missing her more than usual. When she returned home after her trip, they got together for the first time since she'd been away, and her lover had a heart attack and died in her bed the first evening home.
>
> Certainly this man's soul knew he was going to die, and he was just waiting for her to return home. Although the man, consciously,

probably had no idea why he was making those unusual phone calls or that his time in this life was reaching an end.

If you've read any of the accounts of people who died at the World Trade Center, you may have noticed that many of them, like one woman who was on Flight 11 from Boston, seemed to behave in ways that would indicate they had some sense of what their fate would be.

This woman, as her husband reported, left her home in a Boston suburb at 5 A.M. to catch her flight. But before she left, she insisted on waking their two small children and kissing them goodbye. "Thank God she did," her husband said afterward.

By the same token, I've always been fascinated by the story of Leon Klinghoffer, whom you might remember was a passenger on the Achille Lauro, a cruise ship that was taken over by members of the Palestine Liberation Army some years ago. Mr. Klinghoffer was confined to a wheelchair, and by all reports, he refused to cooperate with the terrorists and taunted them verbally until they pushed him over the side of the ship to his death. He was the only passenger to die as a result of that hijacking, and I've always wondered what caused him to behave as he did.

Anyone with any sense knows that you don't antagonize armed terrorists and expect to survive the experience. The mindset in a situation like that is to make a statement, and is governed by the use of fear. Did his soul know that it was his time to die? Did his soul *want* to pass over at that time? Was this his way out of the wheelchair existence in which he had been confined? I know there must have been a reason for his seemingly risk-taking behavior, and I believe his soul must have known that reason even if his conscious mind did not.

we, too, have a job

An individual's soul always knows its program even though we, on a conscious level, may not. And just as it's the job of the DPs to communicate with us and let us know what they are doing and what they have to do, it's our job to try to determine what it is we need to be learning and to try to make choices that will help us to grow so that our soul can move on to the next stage of its eternal evolution. In the greater scheme of things, I think we are not *only* here to be *doing* something with our individual Soul Programs, we are here to learn to *be* something through the lessons of our Soul Programs. If you are not bringing yourself forward into some kind of outward expression of manifestation then you are not taking advantage of your soul's journey into reincarnation for evolution.

How many of us have found ourselves at some point in our lives when we were engaged in something that we really didn't want to be doing or heading in a direction we knew we didn't want to go? Some place or direction that deep down inside we knew had nothing to do with who we are. On a lot of levels it creates a more difficult life for us that can be difficult anyway. I would say more than a few. One of the themes I hear about continually, while out on tour, comes as a result of the events of 9/11 in the United States. It seems that people are changing the direction of their lives in dramatic ways—leaving a job they haven't enjoyed for years, taking time to be with family more, and not working so many days/hours so they may have more time for the simple things they enjoy. Now that is a wake-up call on a huge level.

I love what Oprah said once on her show. "I believe that you are here to become more of yourself and live your best life." She went on to say that the greatest gift we can receive while on this earthly journey is to learn "*Who*" we are with a capital "W." Makes sense to me. When we are not on course with our Soul Program, we get all kinds of wake-up calls about the earthly paths we may pursue that are out of alignment with what our "true" Soul Program is laid out to be. If there is an issue or pattern that is seemingly wearing you out or seems always in your face, so to speak, wouldn't it make sense that your soul is signaling you that this one needs to be dealt with? I don't think we have to search very far to recognize and understand the lessons our soul has chosen to pursue as its learning program.

We are also given a conscience. Other than having the DPs as support, the conscience acts as a sort of Boundary Program for humans. It helps us keep ourselves in check from entering into any areas that would throw us out of alignment with the "true self," sending us off course, and ending up tainting our soul. We all know in that innermost place when we are doing something or heading in a direction that *feels* out of sorts with ourselves. To not be "in sync" with ourselves is a terrible feeling. I know you understand what I am talking about here.

When we know we are out of sync and continue to head in that direction, we can sometimes do irreparable damage to our soul, not to mention the mind/body/spirit. It eventually will eat away at our self-respect throwing us into a spiral downward. There is most definitely a climate that reveals to those in the medical field a connection between all aspects of the *Self* and how they are interwoven to a point where when we do injury to one, the other is affected. This was ever so present in a medical conference last November in Hawaii where I was a featured speaker lecturing on the connection of depression, anxiety, and grief on the body and how it can result in stroke and heart attacks. I am excited about how to medical practitioners are opening up to the body/mind/spirit connection. Even though this was basically a medical conference supported by one of the largest hospital research institutions of the world, and I was in a way the 'outsider,' my lecture was so hugely attended that I have been asked back again this year.

There are plenty of escapes we can pursue while "in the body." Once we have left the body, there is nowhere that is an option for escape. So, whatever is revealed to you as an issue or pattern that needs to be worked on, take advantage of the gift of time you have here and those around you that are placed in your path and existence to help. Why build additional negative karma?

chapter six

the grieving task

DINO'S STORY

It was fall. Dave, a friend of mine from work (we're both lawyers), wanted to loan me a copy of Suzane's book. I had never heard of Suzane at that time. I read the cover and thought that the book was too way-out. But Dave insisted it was worth the read. He explained that he just happened to catch Suzane on the radio while he was away on vacation and thought she was inspirational. Later, Dave went to a lot of trouble to track down the book. I appreciated all that and accepted the book from Dave, basically so as not to offend him. I put it on a shelf in my office, figuring I'd return the book someday without ever having read it. This just wasn't for me.

December came and my aunt passed away. I went with the extended family to the burial at a cemetery out on Long Island. That also happened to be where my infant son at two weeks of age had been buried seventeen years earlier. I had been too devastated to ever visit my son's grave before, but I felt a real pull to visit him on the day of my aunt's funeral. Yet, I resisted the feeling that day and for a few days thereafter, never going. Then I started having "visions" of someone or some thing beckoning me to pay a visit to my son's burial place. Simultaneously, for some reason, I also began "seeing" my son with a little girl his own age and kept wondering what that was about. I wasn't aware of spirit guides or DP contact at the time, and so I hadn't a clue as to what might have been happening to me. I began to question my own sanity but, nevertheless, resolved to visit my son's gravesite.

The following Friday night, I bought a nice floral arrangement from a neighborhood florist and drove out to Long Island very early the next day. It was almost dawn when I got there. The fog was dense and eerie, like out of a Stephen King movie. Nobody else was around.

Over, around, and in-between the graves I walked, following the cemetery markers. I began the approach to my son's gravesite, 17 years of repressed emotion coming to the fore. As I got closer, the force that had brought me to the cemetery appeared elf-like on a road in my mind's eye and skipped happily away. I walked on to my son's grave, read the epitaph and started to cry violently, apologizing over and over for not visiting him sooner. I set the flowers down upon the grave and started to leave. I felt a pull to the left and followed it. Two markers over was the grave of a girl named Jennifer who was born and died on the same day. I somehow knew that Jennifer was the little girl I had "seen" with my son, and that he was in some way caring for her. I removed a couple of flowers from my son's arrangement and placed them upon Jennifer's grave.

I started to leave but was overpowered by a need to go back. I returned and resumed crying and apologizing to my son for not visiting him sooner. Suddenly I heard a voice say "What's the matter, Dad?" and in my mind's eye I saw my son appear out of what I can only describe as infinity. He looked to be 17-years-old, but I knew it was him.

"I'm sorry I never came to visit you," I said again and again.

"That's alright, Dad. That's alright. Don't worry."

And with that, I felt forgiveness.

In my car driving home, I again questioned my own sanity. The more I analyzed what had happened, the crazier I felt.

At work the following Monday, I picked up the copy of the book that Dave had loaned me months before and started to read it that night. Suddenly I didn't feel insane anymore. All Suzane wrote about hit home, especially the part where she mentions that babies grow up on the other side. That really struck a chord. "That's why he was 17 when I saw him," I said to myself.

Soon thereafter, I learned that Suzane would be holding a seminar in nearby New Jersey. I went and was intrigued by every aspect of the event: the lecture, the questions and answers, the meditation, the mini-readings, and of course, by Suzane herself. I attended a second Suzane seminar in Manhattan, and another one a few months later, back in Jersey.

By the third seminar I pretty much new what to expect and had become very relaxed. At the first couple of seminars I actually had feared that Suzane would read me, but later came to think that she never would. Then during the readings portion of the third seminar, Suzane came charging over to the area where I was seated. "Who lost a child over here?" she asked. I didn't answer. "Come on, somebody lost a child here. This is very strong." Again I didn't answer. Suzane tried to leave but came back saying, "He's not gonna leave me alone. Is it Brian? It's Brian. Who knows a Brian?"

That wasn't my son's name. But no one was claiming Brian, so I finally answered, "Is it Ryan?"

Suzanne snapped her fingers and her face lit up. "That's it!" she said and proceeded to tell me that Ryan wanted me to know he was alright. Through Suzane, Ryan added that his sister with the "K" name wouldn't let him go. The "K" identification was right on but I was still somewhat skeptical, for I had no idea whether my older daughter in fact could not "let go" of her brother. Suzane continued, "He also visits his sister with the 'M' name." Whether these visitations were occurring, again I didn't know, but my younger daughter does indeed have an "M" name. Then Suzane stood right in front of me and asked, "Did he die of cancer?" I indicated not. Suzane asked, "Then why is he showing me this?" as she tied an imaginary rope around her neck and lifted it up as if she were being hung.

I replied, "That's because his death was ultimately a result of being choked during birth by the umbilical chord. He never recovered and died at two weeks." And in that moment I knew, not just believed, but knew that there was life after death, and that my son was indeed okay on the other side. The remaining grief and guilt I still was harboring vanished in an instant, and the questions I had about my own sanity also disappeared, for the most part.

"You have a very strong son," Suzane told me after the seminar, and I was just so happy to hear her say that, I couldn't help but ask, "What?" Suzane looked me in the eyes and stated, "I said, you have a very strong son."

I thought, "Yes, I do. Have, not had. Have."

Soon after that magnificent mini-reading, I started to become active on Suzane's internet message board, helping to answer questions and share experiences with all those who visit there. It's been about five years now and I'm still there, pretty much every day, looking for opportunities to pass along the knowledge that Suzane has brought us, along with all the healing that accompanies that knowledge. I've gone to many of Suzane's seminars and workshops over the years, plus one séance, and the results are always staggering not only for me, but also for the people I bring with me, and so many others in the audience.

I ask myself, "Was it by mere coincidence that Dave just happened to catch Suzane on the radio that time, and buy the book, and persuade me to take it? And that I, in turn, would find such a complete degree of healing from the book and Suzane herself that I would become very active on her board and in my own circles, working to help others achieve the same kind of healing from Suzane and her teachings that I have experienced? Was this all just mere coincidence?" And the answer I get is, "No. No coincidence."

Even knowing that death is a transition rather than an end doesn't mean that we won't grieve for the loved ones we lose. In fact, we have to grieve; we have to mourn before we can arrive at any kind of resolution and "let go." Sometimes we also need to forgive or to reach a new level of understanding. But whatever grief work there is for us to do, it's always part of our Program.

Grief work is a term used by professional counselors, who know that the grieving task is never easy. In my work, I also understand the value of what working through our grief does to help us learn the lessons our soul needs to, and must learn, to master loss and sorrow in order to move on. How we deal with our grief and come to terms with our loss and sorrow is a reflection not only of who we are, but also of who the DP is and what he or she meant in our lives.

While the initial loss may be harder when we've had a loving relationship with someone on this plane, it's often easier in some degree to accept his or her passing than it would be if the relationship had been a difficult one. As one of my clients wrote after she attended one of my seminars, "I don't feel better about my Grandmother not being here with me, but at least I know now she is happy and well and with my Grandpa."

This woman's grieving task was pretty straight-forward. There was no anger to prevent her from finding comfort in the knowledge that her grandmother had made a peaceful transition; there were no "issues" left to be resolved. Perhaps the only lesson this woman needed to learn was the essential "fact" of her beloved grandma's continued existence in the world of spirit.

And, of course, there are those relationships where someone is "at odds" or estranged from a person they love at the time of their passing. Those situations in relationships have a definite impact on the grief work to be done. Here's an example:

> I attended an evening seminar of Suzane's in hopes of hearing from a dear friend that had passed within the last six months. This had been a huge loss for me since, over the past 20 years, we had a relationship that had gone from friends to lovers and

back to friends. It was a bond that I have rarely seen anywhere else—except in the movies. Mark and I knew each other so well, and were each other's confidants. I was having a hard time moving through the pain and guilt I was carrying to even begin the grieving process. In the months before his death, I had become involved with another man, and became so wrapped up in that situation, and afraid to tell Mark that I had put off making any kind of time to get together, giving some excuse or another each time he would call. I felt he had to be present in some way still because we once committed to sticking around in order to help the other out in life in case one would pass on before the other. I needed to know if he was present and knew how sorry I was that I hadn't seen him before his death.

Early in the evening, as Suzane stepped off the platform and came into the audience to deliver messages, she came right over to my section and was talking to a woman in front of me and gave a name that this woman identified with. Now, the odd thing was that most everything she was telling this woman about the DP who was present, could have been the exact things if she had been talking to me about Mark. I wanted to raise my hand and say, "I think those messages are for me." My hesitation came in the fact that the name Suzane got was far from being my friend's name—nowhere near.

As Suzane moved on to another section and into the rest of the evening, I sat obsessed with the information she had given this woman—I am here, I love you, I am well, move on, and don't feel guilty—

rolling over and over in my mind. Why hadn't she come to me? Why didn't Mark come through? This was so like him talking. All that she had said to this woman was what I needed to hear and wanted to hear from him. The woman was quite moved and seemed to get great comfort from the messages delivered. She seemed so frail at first, yet as I glanced over to her from time to time over the rest of the evening, her body went from a collapsed position into straight up as she listened intently to the rest of Suzane's deliveries to others in the room. There obviously was some sort of shift going on inside her.

Right toward the conclusion of the evening, Suzane said something that was to have great importance and impact for me. She said that sometimes a DP we want to contact, or have contact us in a group situation, will step back to let another DP come through with the same message they want to deliver to us because "the other person" needs to hear it more and so it is directed at them. She then said we are to learn to listen in a different way than what we have been used to. I now believe Mark was stepping back, yet letting me know through this woman's message what he wanted to say. Driving home that night, I decided Mark did know I was sorry and he was around. It was time for me to grieve and move on—so we both could move on.

The story above gives example how one person, even though the message was not directed *to* her, made a conscious choice to take the information of the message that appeared to be an underlying message *for* her, and came to a conclusion to move on in a leap of faith to begin her own transition into healing and closure. This also illustrates that everything happens for a reason. She was there and got a message. Was her friend, Mark, there participating? I think so. Too often, however, it isn't that easy to find closure or to come to peace with death, and sometimes we just make it more difficult for ourselves because we simply don't want to hear what the DPs have to tell us.

holding on to anger never does any good

Anger is like a brick wall. Sometimes it can be built so strongly that it would take a bulldozer to bring it down. Many times I have seen anger set so deeply that the true message of a DP has no chance of coming through. Such is the case exhibited in the session that follows.

A couple sat across from me on the couch. He was rigid with anger and she was rigid, too, but I could tell that hers was the kind of rigidity that indicates holding oneself together to avoid hysteria. I felt a little girl's presence—sweet and shy and loving. She told me her name was Jennifer and that her sister had been there to meet her, which also let me know that the couple sitting before me had had to cope with the deaths of at least two children. No wonder there was so much emotion in the room.

I felt that she had died of cancer, which Jennifer confirmed, and then her father validated. As he said gruffly, barely moving his lips, "Yes, it was cancer," I could sense the little girl stepping forward, hesitating, and then stepping back. That happens. It's an emotional surge and withdrawal. The child had stepped forward to comfort her father, but pulled back when she felt the extent of his rage.

For more than 30 minutes that rage poured out. Anger at God, at life, at other people who had healthy children and hadn't had to go through what he'd gone through. When the older daughter, the couple's first, stillborn child and the one who had brought Jennifer over, also came through that afternoon, she, too, was met with rage.

"Stop him," I felt Jennifer say. "Remind him of my brother at home who is so unhappy."

I tried to convey her message, but her father simply didn't want to hear about the living son he still had. All he wanted to do was rail against whatever power had taken his daughters from him.

As the session continued, I felt more and more battered by the anger that was surging through the room. And then, abruptly, it ended. In the middle of his vitriolic diatribe, the man got up, helped his wife, who had remained virtually silent throughout, to her feet, and thanked me politely for letting them know their daughter was no longer in pain.

You could have blown me over with a feather when he stopped at the door, turned, and told me bluntly that he and his wife were planning to adopt another little girl and, goddamnit, she had better be healthy. He wasn't going to go through "this" again.

This tortured father was too angry to listen to what his daughter wanted to say. She'd been trying to offer him solace and a way to build a future with his son. But he, apparently, had come to that séance just so he could yell at the medium. I guess I seemed like the closest thing to whatever "power" he'd decided had taken his child from him.

I hope it made him feel better because he'd certainly missed out on the opportunity Jennifer had offered for him to begin dealing with his grief and get on with the grief work and his healing process. I don't know what was in that man's Program (I may be a psychic but I sometimes also lose my car keys), but I'd be willing to bet it had something to do with anger management. I just hope he won't have to lose yet another child in order to learn the lesson his soul needs in order to move on.

It is important that we learn how to let anger up and learn how to release it. When we hold onto anger, as you can see from the story above, it only serves as a powerful block to our healing, resolution, and transition.

when you listen, you might learn something

In the HBO special, *Life After Life*, Dr. Risa Gold, a psychiatrist, stated that grief has a beginning, middle, and end. *After-Death Communication*, she went on to say, implies a belief system not all people have, but the experience of being contacted by a dead loved one is known to psychiatry and very common among people who are grieving. That kind of heightened perception is part of the normal grief reaction, and seeing a medium can aid the grief process.

Although most of them don't talk about it very much, particularly in their own circles, there's a kind of underground pipeline through which many traditional therapists do turn to people in my profession, myself included, when they can't help a patient resolve issues he or she might have around death. Therapists, needless to say, know how to deal with the living, but dealing with the dead (and accepting that the dead aren't really dead) isn't something they've been trained to do. Since they can't "talk" to the dead person, they can't help their very-much-living patient cope with the problems he or she might have with a person who communicates on a different level. And some of them are, therefore, open-minded enough to refer the patient to someone who can.

Not too long ago, in fact, a therapist referred a patient to me because she couldn't provide the answers that would allow him to move on following the death of his lover. Her patient was gay and had met a man with whom he had a phenomenal connection. Tragically, however, his partner developed AIDS shortly after they got together, and from that point on, their relationship was all about dying. Now that his lover was dead, the surviving partner began to doubt that there had been any relationship between them beyond that which revolved around the disease.

The therapist could reassure her patient as much as she wanted, but he still needed to *know*. After just one session with me, during which his lover, of course, came through and validated the depth of his feelings for the sitter, assuring him that they're love was *not* simply based on a caregiver/patient relationship, the grieving partner was able to move on, and effectively turn his entire life around. It's not that he missed his lover any less, or that he wasn't still saddened by the loss. It was simply that, after their communication, he could be confident that what he'd felt there was between them was real and not merely some kind of wishfulfillment on his part.

It's certainly heartening to be able to help people referred to me by mainstream therapists, but I don't require that kind of validation to know, absolutely, that communicating with the DPs can have a salutary effect on our grief. I get my validation every day from clients like the woman who wrote:

> Both my parents have passed away, my mother, with whom I was closest, 16 years ago, my father more recently. Since my mother's passing I'd grown very close to my father, and his death really put me in a tailspin.
>
> I went to this [séance] hoping to connect with my father, just to know he was out there and okay. My mother is the one who came through the strongest. She's taking care of him now, so I'm happy about that. I feel I can move on now.
>
> Because of my experience with Suzane, I have happiness in my heart again. She really taught me that the love and the family connection never go away.

To profit from our communication, however, it's necessary that we *listen* to what the DPs have to say, because their messages are always for our benefit. Sometimes it's just our reluctance to believe in the Soul's survival that prevents us from being receptive to the messages our loved ones are trying to deliver. For the gentleman I described who had lost two daughters, anger was the blocking agent. But sometimes the DPs are simply trying to tell us something we just don't want to hear.

One woman who came to me was so
upset over her daughter's death that she'd
transferred her grief into a compulsive shopping habit. Every week she could be found in
some mall or outlet center compulsively buying and buying. Her closet began to look like
the racks in a department store with all the
tags still on. Rarely did she even bother to
wear any of her purchases. Some of the items
weren't even in her size. She had done this so
religiously over the months since her daughter's
death until she was not only substantially in
debt, but also in denial of her problem.
Needless to say, this had put quite a strain on
her relationship with her husband. From what
their daughter in spirit told me, it had been
their love for her that kept them together in
the first place, and now that she was gone
they'd begun to drift farther apart.

During our session, the young girl tried
to talk to her mother about the spending
problem, but she just kept changing the subject. The daughter was pretty persistent, but
the mother was even more so. All she wanted
to hear was that her daughter was safe and
well and that she knew how much she was
missed. She didn't want to know that the
daughter had her own opinion about where
her missing her was leading, or that she
wanted to advise her mom about the com-
pulsion she saw growing out of denial. That

was not the kind of relationship this mom wanted to have with her daughter—either on this plane or the next.

The death of a loved one can be a real wake-up call, providing important insight into the trajectory of our own journey. Yet, only if you are willing to listen to *whatever* might come through with an open mind. To profit from that insight, however, we need to deal with the issues that surface during the grieving process. If we turn our backs on those issues and that process, we will be passing up a prime opportunity for growth. The woman with the compulsive shopping problem never came back, so I never was able to find out how her life was going, but I got the feeling when she was there that it couldn't be going anywhere good.

If we do listen, however, as in the case below, it can make all the difference:

An attractive young woman came to me looking ill and worn out, and when she explained, between deep, breathy sobs, that she'd opened the front door one night to find her father, with whom she lived, literally dying on his own doorstep, I could understand why she was so tired and emotionally drained.

It seemed that he'd gone out to the ATM machine one night to get some money, calling "Back in a minute" as he went out the door.

But thieves, apparently, had followed him home and killed him at his own doorstep, for the cash, just moments before he would have reached safety.

For weeks afterwards, the family had "felt" his presence in the house but didn't know what to do about it. The daughter was enduring severe headaches and, one night, too restless and headachy to sleep, she went down to her father's study and decided to play some music. By "coincidence," she put on some CDs of old Frank Sinatra and Tony Bennett songs. She couldn't say why she'd made that choice. It wasn't her type of music at all, but those songs had been her father's favorites. As she sat there in a kind of reverie listening to the music, she heard her father's voice. They chatted a bit, and then his spirit departed. "I felt him smiling," she told me. "I know how wonderful I felt when he used to smile at me, and this was the same."

Although she still senses her father's love around her, he's never returned in the same way. But it's enough for her to know that he's at peace, and her headaches have never returned.

it's still your choice

If you look back at the last few pages, you'll see that in no instance did the DPs, who communicated with their loved ones, actually interfere with the living person's exercise of free choice. It's always up to us to decide whether or not we're willing to hear what they have to say. And then we still have to decide whether or not to act on the strength and direction of their messages. But, as I've already said, the DPs always have our best interests at heart. Whatever they want us to hear stems from their eternal love, and, for the sake of our souls, we would do well to at least try to discover what lesson we were meant to learn from having to deal with the grief of their passing.

I'm sure you can see that it would be better to find the peace that young woman discovered listening to music with her father in spirit than it would be to go through life tormented by unresolved anger or to throw away a loving relationship with your surviving spouse, children, or loved ones because grief was causing you to engage in self-destructive behavior.

when issues go unresolved

When we've truly loved someone who's passed on, our grieving is fairly uncomplicated and straightforward. It may be difficult for us to understand why he or she was taken from us or to discover what meaning that death might have for the course of our own journey, but the grief itself isn't wrapped up in a tangle of other, conflicting emotions. That's why, whenever I'm given the opportunity, I advise people to try to work through their relationship problems on this plane, because it's just a lot easier. Certainly the frustrated therapists, who send their patients to me, know that to be true.

When we express pain or anger or disappointment to someone who's living, we simply stand a better chance of getting—and understanding—the answers we need to arrive at peace and resolution. There are several reasons for that. For one thing, I've noticed that death can alter our perceptions of what those relationships were like in ways that are not always useful or "healthy" for the griever.

Some time ago, for example, I met with two women, sisters, whose father had died when they were both in midlife. The older woman was still angry about things her father had done in life, while the younger was loving and forgiving. To listen to their stories, however, one would think those feelings ought to be reversed.

The younger child had been the more outgoing and "dramatic" in every way, and her acting out had, apparently, angered her father on more than one occasion to the point where he actually hit her. Both women agreed that, as a child, the younger sister had been "smacked around a lot." But it was the older of the two, who had not been hit, who was now harboring anger and resentment at behavior she'd only witnessed, while the one who had born the brunt of his physical abuse declared that their father had been "very generous" and had provided them with many luxuries.

The two of them wound up arguing about their mutual past, the older accusing the younger of "writing revisionist history," while the younger berated her older sister for not being more forgiving. It's impossible to know without having been there whose version of "history" was more accurate, but I think it's safe to say that the death of their father had caused both these women to see him differently from the way they probably did in life. Was one better off than the other or were they both, in effect, grieving (or failing to grieve) the loss of someone who was, in fact, a stranger? Without their father there to talk to, the one certainty is that they'd both have a harder time working through their feelings now than they would have if they'd confronted these issues while he was still alive.

Another reason why it can be more difficult to resolve *unresolved* issues with our loved ones in spirit is that The Boundary Program may, for whatever reason, prevent the DP from giving us the answers we seek. I've already talked about how this can work in the case of violent death, for example. And, finally, communication with those in spirit is simply not as straightforward as communication with the living. The DPs send messages that come through as sounds, sensations, feelings, and impressions, but they don't have the same kind of verbal interchanges that we do in the physical body, so it takes more effort for us to understand and interpret exactly what it is they're trying to tell us. And, in addition, the conflicts that remain important to us may not necessarily be important to them anymore. Their love and concern for us continues, but issues that were unresolved when they left the physical body are most likely no longer issues for them. They may simply have moved beyond their anger or disappointment or emotional pain and, therefore, be unable to provide what *we* need to move beyond ours.

The following exchange, posted on the message board of my Website a couple of years ago, illustrates just how difficult it can be for us here to come to terms with our feelings for those who have passed.

Mary,

You hold such anger within you. I did too. My mother can only be politely termed disturbed. Her heart is twisted and she's caused my sisters and me enormous pain—physically, verbally, and worse still, emotionally. She also manifests a lack of care for life. Her emotions seem subdued one minute and volatile the next. I lived with her for about five years of my life, which I term "The True Horror Years." I truly despised my mother. I wanted absolutely nothing to do with her, until I began to find out about the person my mother was besides just my mother. My mother's entire life could be termed "The True Horror Years."

At first I didn't care. Why should what she went through affect me? I didn't do anything to her. She shouldn't have done anything to me. But, life isn't easy, and unfortunately most people don't have the strength, mentally, to live that kind of situation out the best they can. My mother had buried immense pain and turmoil deep within. So deep that when it surfaced, it created an agony that most nearly resembled two people warring within herself. No one knew. Maybe no one cared. She learned to exist with it, but she had no skills to do this well.

No, my mother shouldn't have had pets, much less children. But she did. And I chose her to be my mother. Yes, I chose her. I believe souls know who they are going to be born to. They know their strengths and weaknesses—they don't choose at random (at least I don't think they do). We are born into the world ready to learn the lessons we need to learn, and our birth parents are usually the first ones to aid us along this task. That doesn't mean they'll be great parents. It's impossible if they're not great people.

Unfortunately, it seems neither of our mothers were. Maybe both their souls are scarred from other lives, other experiences. I don't know. I do know that this wouldn't change the fact that they caused us pain. But I believe we should try to work at letting go of the anger. Why should we carry it into another life? The only person that can be hurt by doing that is ourselves. I'm no longer as angry with my mother. I don't see her, I rarely speak to her, and I certainly haven't forgiven her behavior. But I don't hold any overwhelming anger towards her—she's a woman who needs healing and she can only find that from within. I truly hope she does.

I hope your mother has found healing on the other side. And I hope you find healing in this life. I hope we both do.

— Emily

Emily,

You are correct—I still have anger towards my mom even though she died five years ago. I seem to have more feelings towards her when I talk to my brothers, who were terrified of her also. And I also have heard that we "choose" our parents before we are born.

Thank God that I have a great Dad but why did I have to choose such a sad and scary Mom? I wonder if I was a terrible Mom to her in a past life and if this is my punishment in this life. Ever since my Mom died, I have dreams about her. She never says anything to me in the dreams. She just stands near me. Those dreams have helped lift some of the anger towards her. Unfortunately I sometimes have dreams where my mom is her "old angry self."

— Mary

Emily has been lucky enough to understand, while her mother is still alive, not only that she'd done the best she could based upon her own unhappy life, but also that she, Emily, had chosen her mother because her soul needed to learn the lesson that being brought up by that woman could teach. Perhaps it was forbearance or forgiveness; perhaps it was simply to develop her own internal strength. I don't know for sure, but what I do know for sure is that by coming to terms with her own feelings before her mother's death, she's learned enough to spare herself the additional pain of having to live with the guilty feelings that always accompany a lack of resolution.

Mary, unfortunately, has not been so lucky, and her unresolved anger has continued to impact her life even after her mother's passing. In the concluding paragraph of her message to Emily, she speaks of having given up a handicapped son for adoption because "I thought he would hate me as I hated my mom." Emily thought she was being punished for some past transgression, but, as I hope you understand by now, The Soul Program is not about punishment, and Emily has really been punishing herself. She believes God wanted her to give up that child. Whatever you believe, I hope she has been making the choices since that will help to heal her soul and resolve her pain.

but what if they have issues with us?

One might think that just as we may have unresolved issues with those who've passed on, their
issues with us while on the Earth plane also remain
unresolved. Consciousness, as we know, continues
forever; if it didn't, we wouldn't be able to communicate with the DPs as we do. And the learning that
occurs in the physical body is also carried with us
after death. So it stands to reason that while the DPs
remain *conscious* of whatever shortcomings or dis-
appointments they may have experienced in their
relationships with us on this plane, the all-important
difference is that they don't carry over the same emotional attachment we feel when they pass to the other
side. They quickly move through it, and move on.

Once again, any anger, bitterness, resentfulness,
fear, pain, or any other negative emotion you attribute
to the DPs is, in reality, coming from you. Their message is always—and I can't emphasize or repeat this
enough—that they love you, they're doing well, and
they're doing what they need to do to continue their
soul's journey. If they were angry with you, all is forgiven, but as part of *your* process, it may take time,
especially if your relationship with them, or theirs with
you, was particularly angry, volatile, or frightening.
If a parent was abusive, for example, his or her child
might not want to hear from the DP. The child
might, from the beginning at least, refuse to communicate. But that child also needs, eventually, to

resolve his or her anger so that his soul can move on to the next level. The parent's attempt at communication may be just the opportunity the child needs to reach that resolution, even if the child cannot bring themselves to forgive on this level, his or her soul will come to understand, and the parent will eventually receive his forgiveness. The process of forgiveness is different in the spirit world than it is when we're in our physical body, and those left behind, just like the DPs, need to resolve their issues.

In the end, any lack of forgiveness you feel is entirely your own. Part of the task of grieving is to learn to forgive yourself and sometimes others so that you can let go of those negative emotions and move on. It's part of the DPs' job to make your job easier by letting you know you're forgiven, just as it's your job to listen and act upon what they have to say. They can't *make* you move into forgiveness— that's part of *your* Program. But they *can* help to make you aware of the fact that forgiveness might be one of the lessons you're here to learn.

the energy of grief

What flows from us to our loved ones who have passed is vibratory energy, and that energy can be either positive or negative. Until we've learned to work through our grief, resolve our self-defeating emotions, and find a way to get our soul back into balance, we'll be emitting negative energy, and we won't be able to move on with our lives. We'll be building negative Karma, which will have to be balanced at some point, on this plane or the next. No matter how much positive energy the DPs might be sending our way, we have to be open to receiving it and using that energy as they would want us to—to move on to the next stage of our journey so that we don't have to carry accumulated negativity into our next life and learn the same lessons all over again. That's why I call grieving a "task." It's a job we have to do, get through, complete, and set aside; otherwise, it will continue to haunt and hang over us just as any other task that's left uncompleted in our lives. Dr. Elisabeth Kübler-Ross, who counseled hundreds of patients and their families through her research into death and dying, also knew that each stage of grief— denial, anger/resentment, bargaining, depression, and acceptance—carried with it a certain energy. Until we do our grief work and move through the first four stages to that calm place of acceptance, we will be emitting a degree of resistant energy in all that we do, and the DPs quite often *interpret* this as a sign that you are not ready yet for connection or communication.

chapter seven

how souls
find one another

Several years ago a coworker and friend of mine was going through a crisis. Her stepdaughter had run away from home. My friend was devastated. She was upset all the time, and simply asking how she was doing or if she had heard anything would bring tears to her eyes.

I felt such sympathy for her. Years earlier, my sister had run away from home. My mother was a mess at the time. She was always crying and never sleeping. It went on for several months. Eventually, my sister called, but not long after that my mother developed cancer and passed on.

As I was leaving work one particular evening, I spoke to my friend and again she was in tears. She had no idea where her stepdaughter was, if she was safe, if she needed anything, or if she would ever be home.

Driving home, I turned on the radio in the car to listen to Suzane. It wasn't the first time I'd heard her, but as they say, timing is everything. Anyway, I listened as I drove and by the time I stopped my car I was in tears. I sat in my car for a moment and started talking to my mom. I told her about my friend at work and all that she was going through. I knew my mom would understand because of her similar circumstance. I said to her, "Mom, if what Suzane is saying is possible, then you can hear me, you know what my friend is feeling and how much pain she is in. I can't expect you to get her daughter home, but if you can just somehow relay a message to her daughter to call her mom and let her know she is safe . . ." In my head I envisioned my mom knowing someone who knew someone who knew this young girl, and the message, the *strong* impulse to call being passed to this girl.

Anyway, I went about my evening as usual. When I got to work the next morning I was greeted by my friend, who informed me that her stepdaughter had called the night before and was safe.

the pull of similar vibrations

Souls with like energy do find one another, whether on this plane, the next, or communicating between the two. The woman in the previous story was right when she "knew" that her mother would be able to "get the message" to her friend's daughter that she ought to phone home. Souls with similar programs, similar learning tasks, or similar experiences emanate similar vibrations and "find" one another because they are pulled together by their vibratory energy. What I find is that usually in smaller groups there seems to be a coming together around a theme. In larger groups, it seems that the people that are connected by themes are drawn to sit in the same areas. Energy is a magnet. It happens in my seminars and workshops all the time, as it did when Michael and Terri attended a seminar a few years ago.

> Before we talk about the last seminar we attended, there is a dream I must tell you about. Terri, my wife, was very sick one day. She dreamed that Brandon, our son, was walking by, pulling a red wagon full of babies. Terri called out, "Brandon, it's Mom." Brandon looked at her and told her, "Sorry, Mom, I am very busy right now. There's no time for you right now. I have to take care of the babies," and he continued on his way. Terri woke up and turned on the TV. All the channels were covering breaking news—the Oklahoma City bombing.
>
> When Terri and I attended our last seminar, we walked in to see people we knew, but something

pulled us to sit in a different area. While Suzane was walking through the audience she stopped at our row and said, "There is a BR name," but couldn't explain further. Both my wife and the lady next to her raised their hands. Terri said, "Our son's name is Brandon." The woman next to us said her son's name was Brian. That explained the two conflicting messages. It became clear that both sons were there. Suzane looked at us and said "a large vehicle." We each explained that Brandon was killed by a school bus and Brian was killed by a tractor-trailer. Suzane continued, stating to Brian's mother, "You put large objects on the headstone." She told Suzane that they'd had an airplane put on the stone. Suzane then turned to us and said that Brandon was telling her there were a lot of things in the casket and not enough room for him. We told her we had put in his pillow and sleeping bag, some toys, his dino-snooze, and some pictures of us. After the seminar we talked to Brian's mom, shared pictures, and talked about losing our sons. We told Brian's mom about Terri's dream and she started to cry, telling us that Brian had been killed the day of the Oklahoma City bombing.

Brandon and Brian's parents were drawn together on two levels. The fact that their children were together in spirit obviously pulled them toward one another, as did the fact that they had suffered similar losses and were both emanating similar vibratory energies. Why would Brandon's parents not have chosen to sit with the people they knew at that seminar? Simply because the "pull" of Brian's parents' vibrations was clearly much stronger than the impulse to join their friends.

Another, truly astonishing example of this occurred at a recent seminar when two couples were sitting in the same row, across the aisle from one another. Both had lost sons of the same age in car accidents, and both had second sons named Michael. It seemed that each time I received a message it applied equally to both of them. When I asked who had something in his pocket related to his son, the father of one said that he always carried a stone that would remind him of his child while the other pulled out a chain he'd given to his boy and taken from his neck after the accident that killed him. Both couples, it turned out, lived in the same city and had come to the city we were in just to attend my seminar. And, perhaps most remarkable of all, the mother of one had had an extremely vivid and detailed dream in which the other couple's son appeared. She was able to describe him precisely, even though they'd never met and at the time of the dream she had no idea who he was. As the evening progressed, it became more and more clear to me that these two families would be bonded for life because of their similar losses.

There's another example of that vibrational pull that reminded me, when I heard it, of something that might have happened in a wonderful romantic movie like *Sleepless in Seattle* or *An Affair to Remember*, in which the characters' souls—in these cases both couples were actually lovers—seemed to be drawn together by almost impossible coincidence (except, of course, that nothing is ever really *just* a coincidence.) In any case, this is the story as it was reported to me by a woman who had lost both her parents and was embroiled in an extremely difficult and emotionally draining relationship with her siblings.

The year that followed the death of my father was horrible for my relationship with my siblings. All the typical things you hear happen to families when they lose their parents—the horror stories about miscommunication and distrust that you swear could never happen in your own family—were happening in mine.

The pressure was intense and I felt like (and honestly was treated like) an outsider. My siblings were each married and had children. I was not. I felt they had homes and support systems I lacked. Their primary families were still there, in their homes every day. I was alone. During the last year of my father's life I spoke to him almost every day. I saw him, at the very least, once a week. His passing left a huge void in my life, and when I turned to my family for support, I got only anger, frustration, and more problems. (To be fair, they were also recovering from a great loss, and I'm sure it was easy for each of us to see why we hurt the most and were left with the least.)

Anyway, as Thanksgiving was approaching, I knew I couldn't do the "family thing." It was just too difficult and after the horrible year I'd had, the pressures were too great. I knew it would be a recipe for disaster. My niece was spending a semester in Rome, so I decided to take a ten-day tour of Italy, including a visit with her. The trip was a gift from my dad (from his inheritance) but became an even more important gift.

On Thanksgiving Day I happened to be in Florence. I was spending the afternoon on my own and decided to stop at a café for my first taste of gelato. In line in front of me was a man about my age, also an American. We talked for a bit while we waited and then continued our conversation in the square. He asked what I was doing in Florence on my own on Thanksgiving, and I explained that my father had died the year before and I'd just needed to get away. He said, "The same with me, except it was my mom. I'm single and my brothers and sisters are married, and they just don't understand what I'm going through." I said, "Same with me. It's been horrible, and they treat me as if I'm a child and don't have any say in anything." And he said, "Same with me, and to make it worse my dad died almost ten years ago." "Same with my mom," I said. And so it went.

Imagine two people going through the same thing, with the same issues and the same reactions and the same needs, bumping into one another in Florence while waiting in line for gelato on Thanksgiving Day; two people who would normally be with their families.

We spoke for a while longer and then went our separate ways. I don't know who he is or even exactly where he's from. We didn't exchange names or numbers. But I do know that meeting him changed my life. I was no longer alone. I never spoke to him again, but when things get rough with my family I know he's out there somewhere and I'm not alone. I was able to go home and see my family, and it didn't hurt so much anymore when I was left out or when they didn't call to see if I was okay, because I knew two things—one, he was out there somewhere going through something that is very similar, and that is somehow very comforting. And, two, my parents were (and are) still around. They are still taking care of me and making sure I am okay. Meeting this man (although sometimes I do wonder if he was an angel) saved my spirit and was the best gift my parents could have given me.

While the vibrational pull of those suffering similar losses may be the strongest kind of bonding glue, the fact is that anyone who has suffered a loss and is trying to communicate with a loved one in spirit will be to some degree drawn to others who are doing the same. That's why when I do retreats or cruises, during which clients are, of necessity, together for an extended period of time, those events are always bonding experiences, and can also be healing simply because everyone there is more or less "in the same boat," either literally or figuratively, and they can provide solace and comfort for one another. Sometimes, in fact, I'm sure the DPs arrange it that way.

the DPs know
where they're needed

Our soul always knows where it needs to be, and because, as science has now taught us, energy exists at all points in the space-time continuum simultaneously, it's possible for the DPs to "appear to be" in more than one place at the same time—if that's what we need of them. Here's what happened when a woman came to one of my seminars in Connecticut hoping to hear from her grandma:

> The day of your seminar was a jumble and I got hopelessly lost despite stopping for directions three times. I arrived about 20 minutes late, just as you were ending your introduction and explanation of what you do. Luckily, I had gone to a workshop a few months before and had heard what I had this day missed. I wrote my gram's name, Rose, on the slip of paper and hoped.
>
> When you had everyone in the room speak about who they had seen at the gazebo [during the meditation] my heart sank a little. My gram had not come to me and I thought my best chance was gone. Little did I know that two people would hear from Rose, both saying that they felt the name before the meditation (right about the time I finally got to the seminar). Rose was in the kitchen, said one lady (whom I hugged after the day was through), wearing her flowered dress and cleaning fish, which she really disliked doing. Her brother, who lived with her and is now in a convalescent home with Alzheimer's

disease, used to love to fish and brought his catch home for her to clean. Oh, how she disliked it.

The woman across the room wrote down "the beach." Gram was always found in the kitchen. She never had a vacation, never traveled to the beach, never wanted to. Then it dawned on me. My mom, Gram's daughter, was at the beach this week. She was on vacation in Ocean City, Maryland. That's why she couldn't come with me that day. Gram must have gone to the beach with her. How happy that made my mom.

Grandma knew where she needed to be, to bring comfort to and acknowledge her continuing presence in the lives of both her daughter and her granddaughter. And, luckily, because God or the Higher Power has arranged it that way, she was able to be with them both. I hope she enjoyed that trip to the beach that she never got to take in life!

The same kind of simultaneous communication occurred on another occasion, when a man brought solace to both a grieving wife and a grieving daughter.

I was so excited when Suzane referred to my husband as Jimmy. I'd been to other psychics, but none of them had ever said his name. She described his favorite red and black plaid jacket and confirmed that he had died of cancer. I left her so excited, knowing that Jimmy was still with me. I was concerned that he would forget me. More importantly, while he was dying I'd been concerned that his daughter would forget him.

The next day, when I awoke, my daughter told me that she'd had a dream about her daddy the previous night. She didn't know I was at a séance with Suzane. I asked her what Daddy looked like and she said, "like Daddy." I then asked her what he was wearing in the dream. She said, "a red and black plaid jacket." I was convinced that my Jimmy had visited his daughter while Suzane brought him through. I know in my heart that he's waiting for me and that he will never forget us!

sometimes our paths need to separate

Earlier, I talked about the fact that families don't *necessarily* remain together after they pass—although there is always at least one loved one around to help us over, and family members are there to communicate with us when messages need to be delivered. But whether or not souls *remain* together or find one another once they've passed depends upon their individual programs.

Since no two souls have exactly the same program, DPs may or may not remain part of each other's journey in spirit. If they still have something to teach one another they will. Or they may become part of another soul's journey, as Brandon, in the story I told earlier, clearly did when he helped bring over the babies who died in Oklahoma City. Children, incidentally, also have tasks to complete, and helping other children adjust to their lives in spirit is very often one of them.

Sometimes, on the other hand, we need to stay together because our Program requires it. And if that's what is required, it will happen. In fact, the lessons we have to teach one another cannot be completely learned without the use of our physical bodies from time to time, it's possible that if one soul reincarnates, the one he or she needs to be with on this plane will reincarnate as well. But that's not always possible either, because one of those souls may have some unfinished business that doesn't involve the other. And, if that's the case, we'll find another person after we reincarnate who can teach us that same lesson. It seems to me the rules get set, and just when I think they have concretized they get reset again. Ah, what an ongoing test against being rigid. Remember that it's not always one particular person we need in our life but the lesson that a certain person has to teach. There are situations, in fact, when we've been trying to resolve issues or learn a lesson from another soul and simply haven't been able to get it right, despite long and hard efforts. If that's the case, and if continuing to do the same thing over and over seems to be getting us no where, the gift of grace will ensure that we'll learn what we need to in some other way. The DPs want those of us they've left behind to make the choices that will help us move on, and the *Power* in charge of the "upstairs team" wants those in spirit to do the same. That's why, whatever any one soul needs to complete some unfinished aspect of its program will occur, one way or the other.

We're always drawn to one another because one of us has something to teach the other, because we both have something to learn, or because the situation created by our meeting will help our soul to grow and move on to the next level of its development. Those lessons may be as various as our programs are unique, but you can be sure there's always a reason.

chapter eight

losing a parent

mothers and daughters, fathers and sons

Choosing our parents is probably the first, and certainly one of the most important, decisions our soul has to make when we are determining how we will come into this life. Who our parents are going to be significantly determines the basic blueprint of our journey. Will one of them die young? Will we be taking care of them in their old age? Will we get along with them? Will they divorce? Will we be an only child? The permutations of how our parents affect the course of our lives could go on endlessly. But *when* a parent dies is one of the most significant elements of all.

The fact that we can never really "get over" a parent's death, no matter when or how long ago it occurred, was brought home to me most forcefully in a letter from a woman who had been on one of my psychic cruises:

> When you spoke my mother's name, Anna, and gave me her message, I thought my heart would stop beating. I was so completely shocked by her name and her message (both of which were so right on) that my senses were completely baffled. Blown away is a good description.
>
> I had never gone to a séance, even though I had always believed in life after death. I was too afraid to go. I tried many other things but never a séance. I guess I trusted you enough to walk into that room.
>
> Never in a million years did I expect my mother, who had died 70 years ago when I was seven and my brother was two, to make contact with me through you. There were two messages and both were so incredibly correct that I'm still shaking my head in amazement.
>
> When I came home, I didn't want to talk to anyone. I just wanted to be alone. I didn't want to read or watch TV. I just lie in my bed and let my body absorb this incredible experience.
>
> Up until that day I had always thought that childbirth was the most intense experience I'd ever

had, but I must admit that your gift of helping people connect was even more special.

That story is particularly moving to me because it validates so many aspects of what The Soul Program is all about. It shows once more that our loved ones are *always* with us, no matter how long they've been gone. It shows how strongly *we* remain connected to *them*. And it makes me wonder, given the intensity of her reaction to their long-delayed communication, in what ways losing her mother at such a young age had affected that woman's life. I don't know, of course. But I'm sure it must have had a profound impact on the course of her journey.

If our parent has lived a good life, well into old age, and if we've had his or her guidance as we grew to maturity, we will, of course, grieve that loss, but it will be a far different grieving experience from that of a person who loses a parent when he, she, or the parent is still young. And this seems particularly true of women who have lost their mothers at a young age.

Shortly after Mother's Day, I happened to be staying at a hotel that delivered courtesy copies of *USA Today* to its guests, and I came upon an article whose opening sentences caught my attention immediately:

> *"My mother died when I was 12, my sister was 2, and my brother was 14," begins Patricia Walsh.*
>
> *"So I became the little mother." That's all it takes.*
>
> *Walsh, who is 67 and lost her mother more than half a century ago, starts to cry.*

The article was describing the meeting of a support group for women who had lost their mothers, and it went on to quote Hope Edelman, the author of the book *Motherless Daughters: The Legacy of Loss,* as saying that "Women lose fathers, women lose siblings, but there's something about the loss of a mother that affects us at a very deep level. There is a real sense of loss of a part of ourselves. We have lost the primary role model for womanhood."

When a woman loses her mother before she's reached maturity, she'll always wonder how different her life might have been if her mother had lived. She might worry that she won't know how to mother children of her own. She might be reluctant to bear children, fearing that she, too, will die young. She might be more resilient and independent than women who had mothers to rely on in their youth, but she also might be less sure of herself because she lacked that essential model of "womanly" behavior. Whatever her reaction to the loss, however, you can be sure that it will have impacted her life on many levels. And if the women who attended that support group meeting are typical, as I believe they are, it will leave a gaping hole that nothing can ever quite fill.

The same, however, can be true for boys who've lost a father. I remember one client especially, whose father had died when he was only nine years old. He'd grown up with no role model for marriage and fatherhood and had worked very hard as an adult to be a good husband and a good father to his own children. When his wife left him and took the children with her, he immediately blamed himself. If his dad had only lived, he kept thinking, he might have been a better husband and father himself. But he *was* a good husband and father, and when his own father came through during our reading, he confirmed that my client had turned out to be just exactly the kind of man his father would have wished him to be. You can imagine the comfort just knowing that brought to this man who had been beating himself up for faults that existed only in his own mind.

A young boy's loss of his father can also impact his life in other ways, as was the case for Ivan, whose extremely conservative and religious father passed away when Ivan was a young teenager. Ivan's mother was left to raise him and his sister with very little money and no other family to fall back on. She moved her family from their small religious community to a larger city with more job opportunities. She worked hard to earn her license as a real estate broker, did very well, and taught both her children to pitch in with chores and to be equally responsible for cleaning the house, getting meals on the table, and washing up. But Ivan, who remembered having been treated very differently when his father was alive, grew to resent the fact that he was no longer the "little male prince." Rather than thanking his mother for having worked so hard to give him and his sister a better life, he blamed her for having shown him a more modern and egalitarian way of living. He left home, returned to the religious community, and never really forgave her for what he considered "robbing" him of the life he believed he'd been intended to lead.

You can experience parenting vicariously by watching the families of friends and seeing how they interact. You can even find a surrogate parent to act as your role model. But you can't experience parenting firsthand if you've lost your parent as a child, and no matter how much love and support you might find elsewhere, your loss will certainly have a significant effect, one way or another, on the way your life progresses.

We've already talked in earlier chapters about two women whose lives manifested the loss of their mothers in negative ways: The one who couldn't seem to find a man willing to commit to a permanent relationship and the other who was literally guarding herself from the approach of others by holding up her arms as if to ward off an attack. Those women knew something was "wrong," as we all do when our lives are simply not going the way we had hoped. They, like the rest of us, had a lesson to learn that would help to put their soul back in balance.

One way to get help when you know you're continuously sabotaging your own chances for happiness is to seek traditional therapy, and I would certainly not discourage anyone in emotional pain from doing that. But, sometimes a mother in spirit can help us to discover things about ourselves that will help to change our vibratory pattern.

Not too long ago, a woman attended first a workshop and then a seminar with me, and the connections she made in those sessions have changed the dynamics of her complicated family life in ways she couldn't previously have imagined.

Kate had been adopted as a baby and, although she knew her birth mother's name, and had made attempts to find her, she'd never managed to meet her in life. At the workshop, her birth mother came through and told her that she'd always loved Kate and her sister, Sandy (whom Kate hadn't met until after their birth mother died), that she was proud of them, and that she was there to help Kate through this time in her life. (Kate was going through a divorce at the time.) Afterwards, Kate said, she felt it was her job "to bring the family back together—my birth family and my adoptive family."

She subsequently attended a séance, unexpectedly, when another participant dropped out, and on that occasion her adoptive father came through along with her stepmother, and her birth mother also returned. Kate asked if they could reveal her original first name, as well as that of her birth sister. The DPs said they couldn't do that but told her that they'd "had to pull a lot of strings for my sister and me to meet. My sister has felt badly that she didn't start searching sooner so she could have met our mother before she died. I have always told Sandy that I don't think it would have been possible for us to meet while she was still alive as I felt that they were helping us. So many things have happened with our family search that were so spectacular I knew I was not doing it myself and that they were helping me and us.

Now Kate has a new man in her life, a man who has eyes of two different colors, as her adoptive father did, and who is in the same business he was. She's also been getting strong "hints" about her birth name in the form of roses.

"After the séance Janet [another participant] and I were driving up to meet a friend of hers. I was talking about my name, wondering if it was Rose, Rosi, or Lili. On my nonidentifying information it is crossed out, and it has been driving me crazy since I first saw it. It looks like it ends in an 'i' and starts with L, P, R, B, D, F, K and is four letters long. As I was wondering aloud what my name might have been I smelled an overwhelming fragrance of roses in the car. I mentioned it to Janet and she smelled it too. There was no air freshener in the car.

"On the drive back I was telling Janet about a man I had met to whom I was strongly attracted. I told her he is very handsome but I didn't notice that at first. I was attracted to the inside first since he is such a kind and thoughtful person. He is the one with the two different colored eyes. He is also in the same type of work as my father, finance. As I was talking about him, I started smelling roses again. I mentioned it to Janet and she said she smelled it too. I felt that this was a good sign that I would *soon develop a very loving relationship with this person.*"

For Kate, being adopted was like losing her mother at birth. She had loved her adoptive parents but that sense of loss, almost a sense of having lost a part of herself (her given name, as well as her birth sister, and her entire birth family) had always been there, a part of her journey. In her case, it was the actual death of her birth mother that allowed her to reconnect with that missing piece, as her birth mother and adoptive parents worked together—again, it's the upstairs team—to help her rediscover what she had lost.

Whether we're consciously aware of it or not, death always affects relationships among the living. In Kate's situation, it was death that brought the family together, but that's not always the case. We've already seen that in the story of the woman whose problems with her siblings sent her to Italy for Thanksgiving, but here is another story that brings the potential problem home even more forcefully:

Ruth was a client of mine for many years. She'd been very close to her father, who had committed suicide when she was a teenager.

Her brother and sister, who were ten and fifteen years older than Ruth, claimed there was no justification for his act, but Ruth, the only child still living at home at the time, understood how much he had suffered both physically and emotionally during his long debilitating illness.

A wealthy businessman, Ruth's father had left his family well provided for. Ruth had been left a large trust fund; her brother, Brad, had inherited his business; and her older sister, Marian, who was married to a wealthy man, had received a substantial sum, but slightly less than Ruth. Her father had made it clear in his will that he had left the extremely profitable business to Brad in lieu of a specific financial settlement and that he felt Marian would be well taken care of by her husband. The siblings, nevertheless, resented Ruth's greater inheritance.

In the years following his death, Ruth's father had made it a point to talk to her about the business so that she could relay the information to Brad, who didn't believe in the DPs, much less our ability to communicate with them. And, after each session, Ruth had dutifully reported his suggestions to Brad, whose only response was, "It's my business now, and I'll run it as I like."

But Brad wasn't "running it" very well. He'd acquired significant debt and the business was now on shaky ground. His father was just trying to help him—as the DPs always do— but Brad was having none of it. The living, as I always say—can be very stubborn.

Meanwhile, Marian's marriage was failing and she was becoming more fixated than ever on the fact that Ruth had inherited more money than she. But Ruth's father was a very wise man, who knew his children's characters well, and he also knew that Ruth would be the one to take care of her mother if the need ever arose.

At the time Ruth last came to see me, her mother had been wheelchair-bound for two years. Her older children, who lived in the same town, had no interest in assuming any caretaking duties. That role fell to Ruth, even though she lived in another state and had to travel several hours each month to pay her mother's bills, take care of business, and sort out any problems that may have come up. Her sister was divorced by then and had become involved with a man who'd managed to spend all her money on himself. Brad had run the business into the ground and filed for bankruptcy.

Ruth's father had, indeed, known his children well and left his money wisely. At our last meeting, when Ruth said she needed to tell her dad what was going on and just vent a little, I told her, "Don't worry, your dad knows. He also knew he could count on you to take care of your mom. You can keep telling your brother and sister that she's their mother, too, but it won't change anything. You've made yourself someone who can be depended on. Maybe that's why your life is so rich—okay, maybe frustrating but also rich—and theirs are such a mess. Your mother knows not to bail them out ever again. She's no dummy. And I shouldn't have to tell you, she loves you a lot."

The death of Ruth's father didn't change the characters of his children. He knew who was who and what was what well enough to make the best arrangements he could for them before he passed. But his passing did bring all their hidden resentments and flaws out into the open. By communicating with him, Ruth was able to understand that she didn't have to feel guilty about her inheritance or about her sister and brother's resentment. Their father had presented each one of them with an opportunity to prosper, both literally and spiritually, but only Ruth had taken him up on his offer. She was doing what she knew she was meant to do. Her siblings, on the other hand, may have to learn that lesson again in another life. And remember that no one was being punished here. Each one of these people had been given an opportunity, and they each reacted to it as they did of their own free choice.

A strong, wise, loving parent can be like the supporting beam for an otherwise shaky structure. Or, as one client wrote me after he and his wife connected with the wife's mother during a phone session with me, "She was a strong bond, and the force that kept my wife's family together." When that beam topples or the bonding glue dries out—or when that one strong parent dies—the whole building might collapse, the bonded material might fall apart, and surviving family members might discover that their paths are suddenly diverging or colliding, rather than running smoothly along the same track. But there's always a reason for that, too. Perhaps it's time for us to "go it alone." Perhaps our parent's death has freed us to discover something about ourselves that his or her protective behavior had stifled or discouraged. Perhaps it's our time to become more mature, more assertive, or simply to make our own way, without parental intervention.

In order to do that, however, we must first learn to come to terms with the death itself. If business between us and the DP has been left unfinished, it becomes much more difficult to move on. A recent message posted on my Website indicates just how that unfinished business can interfere with the course of our own journey:

> My mom and dad both passed during this last year. My mom and I resolved our stuff and I don't feel grief or guilt. I know she is finding her peace as she did here as well. Frustrated and still partly numb, I know that there is work to do around my dad. I am at a loss. I am 40 and have not had a close relationship with a significant other and feel that my undone business will keep me in bondage.

This woman is certainly "in bondage" to her own unresolved feelings, which is why, as I've said, I always counsel people to try to find that resolution while their loved ones are still on this plane—it just makes things that much easier. But, again, I have to emphasize that these are *our* feelings, not those of the DP. That's one of the primary reasons so many people find so much peace in just a single contact with a parent who has passed.

A client of mine recently put that feeling most eloquently:

> In life, my mother was shy, quiet, extremely devout, and not at all comfortable with the "supernatural." I was utterly shocked when my mother was "the first one out of the gate." Suzane described my mom's personality accurately, and the details that came through left no doubt in my mind that she had connected with my mom. My mother spoke about the distance in the family, my father, my children. She acknowledged to Suzane that my son, who was only three at the time of her passing, had seen her twice after she passed. My son had told me this, and Suzane's words confirmed it.
>
> When my mother was dying, the family was with her every day. However, she died one night when we had already left the hospital. Through the years, I have felt tremendous guilt that I was not with her when she died. I should have stayed through the night. I couldn't bear to think of her dying alone.

Before Mom lapsed into a coma, she remarked that her deceased father was waiting for her, and that she could not keep him waiting. During the reading, Suzane said that my mother wanted me to know that she did not die alone, and that the person she said she saw before she died was, indeed, with her when she passed. My mother told Suzane it was important for me to know that she did not die alone. The comfort that has given me is tremendous. I no longer have guilt. The weight has been lifted.

Although I *know* that we never die alone, many people suffer the kind of unnecessary guilt this woman did because she wasn't with her mother when she died. So often the DPs who come through during readings and séances ask me to assure their loved ones that their not being present at the DP's passing was "meant to be" or "as it should be." We pass from this plane to the next as and when we were meant to, and, like the mother in the story above, our soul often knows when that time has come.

If those of us on this plane are able to believe and understand that *everything* happens for a reason, we'll be able to set aside a lot of the guilt, self-recriminations, and other negative feelings we inflict upon ourselves that can unbalance our soul, prevent us from operating within our vibratory pattern, and delay or derail the learning we were meant to do in this life.

chapter nine

parents and siblings:
the loss of a child

losing a parent, especially at a young age, is, without doubt, very difficult, but over the years I've come to understand that there can be no more devastating experience in anyone's life than the loss of a child. Whereas losing an older parent seems for most of us to a be part of the "natural" course of our lives, losing a child—whether it be at 4 or 14 or 40—never seems "natural." It happens for a reason, it's part of our journey, but it's probably one of the most difficult lessons any one of us could ever have to learn.

Having said that, however, I feel I must reiterate that anyone who loses a child has chosen to come into this world as someone who would have that experience. There *is* a reason. If you're a parent, you picked that child. Your soul has chosen its path. If it has been part of your journey, I can't tell you why your soul made that choice, but I do know that you'll find out—if not on this plane then surely between lives.

making contact can help

For many parents, the simple fact that they are able to make contact with their child in spirit and have confirmation that he or she is well, happy, and with other family members is enough to help bring them at least some sense of peace, even in the midst of their grief. But sometimes the child is actually able—if The Boundary Program allows—to provide information the parents could have received no other way.

Just recently—and not coincidentally on Mother's Day—I did a reading for Virginia, a woman who had recently lost Sally, the youngest of her three daughters, in a car accident. After several other relatives had made their appearances, Virginia's mother came through and acknowledged that Sally was with her. What follows is taken from the transcript Virginia sent me of her session along with her explanation of the messages I was receiving:

SUZANE:

Do we know how she passed? I see question marks, which would indicate not all the pieces were put together. I gotta tell you this, though, I feel like she wants you to know that some of the things people might have said about her passing were not what they might have thought. Did they think she took her own life? She didn't pass from an accident, right? This was not a vehicle accident. It was? She was driving? Was someone else involved? I'm not getting her totally at fault. What I am getting here is that we don't know all the facts. I don't know what was indicated in terms of the accident, but she seems to feel she was not totally at fault. I do think from what she is showing me that there is someone else involved and that had some effect on what she hit, what happened. I don't know if she was avoiding something or trying to avoid someone or something. The other person involved didn't tell all the truth here. I feel like we are not all telling the truth here.

The truth won't bring her back but it will matter to the family. You must have raised your children to speak their mind or to be principled children. She is strongly wanting her mama to know that she didn't do anything wrong, that's what I'm getting. I am getting a reaction from an action. What I saw was something that was coming at her that either distracted her or caused her to go off the edge. It was someone else's action that created her actions.

VIRGINIA:

Sally pulled into an intersection in her new white Chevy Cavalier into the path of a pickup truck. She was alone and on her way to work, using a country road to avoid the congested interstate. We're not sure what happened. The morning was gray. The driver of the truck was a 19 year old boy and he was driving a camouflage-style truck. There are no witnesses to say if he had his lights on. There were no skid marks at all. She died instantly. Many of the people who know the area where the accident occurred think he might not have had his lights on. We'll never know for sure.

In this case, it appeared that Sally really wanted to set the record straight. The family wasn't sure what had caused the accident. Sally was saying something different from the driver of the truck, and, as her mother pointed out, they will never have solid information or proof of what happened on the road that morning. Nevertheless, it may help them to know that, at least from Sally's point of view—she wasn't at fault. And hearing will surely help them, as she also conveyed to me that day that she's fine, she's cool, and she's doing her thing.

Sally also gave her mother some information about her relationship with her two sisters, which I reproduce here:

SUZANE:

There really is a big thing with this one sister. Who is the one who is struggling a lot? She's talking about . . . I got . . . like inseparable. I felt like the other one was aware of it, but I don't get anything antagonistic about it.

VIRGINIA:

Marcia [the middle daughter] knew Cindy [the oldest] and Sally were more like each other than she was like either one of them, but she loved both of them anyway. No matter what, Sally was her special "little sister."

Sally then gave me a message that only her sisters would understand:

SUZANE:

She's going to give me something. I feel like she wants to talk about something that happened when she was younger—this funny thing. It has something to do with peanut butter. It has something to do with her sisters; that's why she's giving it. It's almost like when they were kids they did things. It literally has something to do with peanut butter. It's her way of wanting them to know the connection, separate from you.

VIRGINIA:

Cindy and Marcia say that they used to sneak into the kitchen when we were out and eat spoonfuls of peanut butter, sometimes pouring Hershey's chocolate on the spoon just to make it extra gooey-good!

Finally, however, there was a special gift from Sally to her mom:

SUZANE:

One last thing I want to say to you. Your daughter wants you to know that she made sure you got this appointment today, and that it would be yours alone, even though her two sisters had originally planned to accompany you. She said, "I pulled some serious strings."

You know, I told her mom, I didn't plan on working this week at all.

I don't know why Sally was in that car that day, but I did get the feeling, during my session with her mother, that her soul had a sense it would not be long on this plane.

SUZANE:

This is going to sound odd. Did she ever talk about living a short life? I feel like she crammed a lot in. Like she lived ten lives in the short time she was here.

Her mother confirmed to me that her daughter had always seemed like "an old soul" who, when she was only ten years old, wrote poetry about her life ending. She was very upset by the World Trade Center tragedy and, shortly afterwards, wrote the following poem, just weeks before her death:

Is there a reason for this chaos, or does chaos define the reason
Is there truth behind your words or did you forget the meaning
Did you look around today and take it all for granted
Did you forget to thank God that you're still here?
You're standing,
But is it on solid ground?
Because if you've been searching your soul, then it's time
    to let the world
Know what you've found
Tomorrow is not a promise, all you have is this moment
And if you don't take it and embrace it then you will never
    own it
My words are meaningless if my actions fail to coincide
And the one who does not succeed is the one who never tried
I will only truly find myself when I am within my own weakness
And it is in realizing the emptiness that gives me the courage
    to seek this
Do I foolishly invest my spirit when I know they can't hear it?
Yet those who continue to fear it will never see the dreams
    I see,
And the one who I painted my face for only knew the
    entertainer in me
Who you are today is the price you paid for what you
    used to want
So stop paying that price because you can never afford
    to stop dreaming
To stop feeling
To stop loving yourself.

The words she wrote could certainly be about her reaction to a terrible international tragedy and the loss of so much life, but they could also be interpreted as an indication of something she, consciously or unconsciously, felt about the brevity of her own life. Did Sally have a premonition that she would pass? I can't know that with certainty, but sometimes souls do.

Not all children in spirit are quite so communicative as Sally (but then again, not all children in life are equally communicative either). Perhaps it was because her passing was so sudden, without any opportunity for arriving at closure or explanation for her family, that she felt the need to explain as much as she did. I find that most children or young people like Sally, who have been exceptional in their communicative skills while here, usually are more expressive when they come through. True to form. Whatever the reason, her mother seemed happy to know that neither Sally's exuberant spirit nor her loving personality had changed, and that she was still very much connected to her loved ones on this plane.

finding solace
in continued communication

While it's true that the DPs' job is often no more than to let us know they're okay so that we, too, can be okay with the fact of their passing, very often when it's a child who has died, that communication will continue simply because the dead child understands that his or her parents are so in need of maintaining their ongoing connection.

Two of the attendees at a recent séance had lost their son in an automobile accident three years before. Afterward, the father wrote this about their experience:

> We have had a number of very successful readings since the loss of our son Adam. I must tell you that before these readings I would never have considered myself someone who would buy into this. I only did it for my wife. She was doing so badly after the death of Adam that I was willing to try anything to help. We had never been involved with a small group reading and were quite nervous. Our concern was that since we had already been blessed with hearing from Adam, we might be put at the back of the line, so to speak. Many have asked why we would continue to sit with a medium after we already knew Adam was okay. My answer is, if we spoke on the phone with our son three months ago, wouldn't we want to call and talk with him again at some time later? I mean, after all, that's all this really is—a conversation with our wonderful son, Adam.
>
> Suzane was not only accurate with the information but she had his personality right on the mark. She made mention that Adam had the gift of gab, was a real pistol, wanted to be center stage to get the attention, and again was quite a talker. That was a perfect description of Adam.

We enjoyed our meeting with Suzane immensely and would encourage anyone who has suffered a major loss in their life to meet with her and bring things to closure. We all need to be reassured that they are in fact okay and will be waiting for us when we are done here.

Adam was obviously a great communicator, but aside from his chattiness, I believe he knew that his parents—and particularly his mother—*needed* to keep up their communication, and that he would continue to validate their ongoing connection. And, in fact, they returned for a second group reading with me some time later.

We were a good 40 minutes into the reading and still nothing. This was our eleventh reading since Adam crossed over and he had not only always come in strong but usually dominated the readings. Then we finally got our normal lead in by my grandfather, who has increased his time with each session. It had been [in previous readings] either him or my wife's dad who did a quick introduction or lead in to Adam—kind of like Ed McMahon bringing on Johnny Carson. Now the moment we waited for was here. Suzane tells us, "There's a boy with him; is this your son?"

Then she began to give us information about recent events. This, we have learned, is their way of showing they're still with us. She says Adam tells of a party we had yesterday and shows her a waterfall.

We had just had a pool party the day before where we all swam and hung out by the waterfall in the pool. Suzane asks who cut off a finger recently? We explained that Jason, Adam's best friend, had just cut off his finger with a saw at his work. She goes on to say that this young man had been having a very difficult time with Adam's passing. She then asks, "Who is Mike?" Mike is the father of Adam's best friend. She says that Adam was very close to this man, which is true. We spoke to Jason the next day and told him what Adam had said, and he explained how much it meant to him as he'd been having a very difficult time the past few weeks.

With these recent events being brought up and names coming in that related to those events, we once again left with the sense that Adam was okay, and that's all we needed to know for now. As a parent who suffers the loss of a child, you never have enough of making sure your child is okay, but this gave us the peace we needed for now.

In those two letters, Adam's parents validated much of what I know to be true about the continuing bond, the ongoing communication, and the kind of reassurance that can make so much difference when a parent loses a child.

they're always still family

One unnecessarily painful consequence of losing a child—and one that I've heard about over and over again—is the fact that when a child dies, the family often loses much of their potential support system as well. Just when they need the comfort of being surrounded by loving friends and family, they find themselves suddenly isolated in their grief.

People don't withdraw because they're lacking compassion. On the contrary, it's usually because they're so overwhelmed by the enormity of the loss that they either don't know what to say or somehow have the irrational feeling that just being too close to people who've experienced such a tragedy will make them more vulnerable themselves. In consequence, they simply stay away from the surviving family, which means they won't have to say anything at all and perhaps the "bad luck" won't rub off on them. I've even been told by more than one of my clients that they see other women ducking out of sight when they run into each other in the supermarket. I can hardly imagine how difficult that must be—first to lose a child and then to lose the people you would most expect to rally around you in your darkest hour. I don't think these foolish, though probably well-intentioned, people realize how much they are actually contributing to compounding the loss and making the grieving task even harder.

But perhaps more difficult still is the fact that even the people who don't withdraw seem to go out of their way to avoid talking about the dead child—as if he or she were no longer part of the family. The parents almost invariably *want* to talk about their child. He or she will always be part of their family, and they need to *feel* that ongoing relationship. Nor does the child want to be forgotten. He *knows* he's still connected to them, and he wants that connection to be acknowledged.

In her recent book, *Love Never Dies,* author Sandy Goodman, discusses how she has learned to make sure that her son, Jason, will always be part of her life and the life of her family and talks about how important it is for every grieving parent to do that, as well as how friends and other loved ones can help. My personal experience with clients and friends only underscores for me how right she is on all counts.

The need to keep that love alive is one of the reasons joining a support group like Compassionate Friends can be so helpful to people who've lost children. At least the other members of the group will understand what they're feeling, and—most importantly— will be willing to share their own feelings as well. If you're reading this, and you know someone who has lost a child, I hope you'll now have some better understanding of how you can help, and how your actions or inactions can unintentionally compound the loss. (And the same, incidentally, holds true for those who've lost spouses and find that their friends, who had always thought of them as a couple, now shy away from the grieving widow or widower just when he or she needs them most.)

the favorite child,
the replacement child ...
and what about the siblings?

When there's more than one child, parents often have to consider the needs of their living children, even in the midst of their grief. Sometimes it's possible for them to become even closer to a surviving child or children, and they experience the loss together. That's the way it was for Marilyn:

> My story began [almost three years ago], when I lost the most precious person in my life, my beautiful son, Charlie. Charlie was very quiet, and the kindest, sweetest person I have ever met. He was an identical twin to Mark.
>
> I heard about your workshops and asked Mark if he wanted to attend, to see if Charlie would try to get a message to us. We were afraid he wouldn't come through to us because of his shyness. That afternoon when you started to talk about a young boy, I knew you were talking about my Charlie. When you started to tell us about two guys Charlie was with, it didn't make any sense to me, but then you described them, and they were two young boys who are buried in the same cemetery as Charlie. When you said one had a hat, I couldn't believe what I was hearing. The boy you were talking about has a baseball cap bolted to his stone. Then you mentioned leukemia, and I said that was not how he died, but you said no, not him, the other boy died that way.

It did bring me some peace to know he was in the company of boys his age. Actually, I said to Mark on the ride home, all we do is cry and Charlie is hanging out with his friends. It made us both smile.

I want to thank you for all you have done for Mark and me. We spend every day thinking about Charlie. The visit with you made me believe that he was happy. I really didn't believe he could be happy without his brother and me. It didn't make my heartache any easier, but when I sit at Charlie's grave, I always think of our meeting that afternoon.

Marilyn and Mark were clearly joined in their grief, and were able to provide sympathy and support for one another in their mutual loss. When you consider how much more difficult it must be to lose an identical twin than it is to lose any other sibling, it becomes clear how much harder it would have been for Mark without his mother's ongoing concern. But even so, when I received Marilyn's letter, I couldn't help noticing her words: "I lost the most precious person in my life." Did she mean that Mark was somehow less precious than his identical twin, Charlie? And if Mark was aware of those feelings, or if he read her letter, how did that make him feel?

I can't even remember how often parents have told me it was their favorite child who died. It doesn't seem to matter if it's the eldest, the youngest, or the middle child, it's almost always the favorite. People have asked me whether I really think it's the favorite or whether that child only *seems* to be the favorite because he or she has died. I'm sure there's some psychological validity to the idea that whatever you lose seems more precious just because it's gone. We do, after all, seem always to lose our favorite pair of earrings or to leave our favorite umbrella behind in the restaurant. But in this case, I believe these people are being absolutely sincere and honest when they tell me the pain of their loss is all the more difficult because it is their favorite child who's gone.

When an only child dies, the grief for the parents may be the hardest of all. But when a child dies leaving surviving siblings—especially when the parents make it clear that the one who died was their favorite—that loss will surely have serious effects on the surviving children and on the dynamics among all the surviving members of the family. Will the remaining children feel guilty for having lived? Will they be angry with their parents for loving them less? Will they feel neglected because their parents are so involved in the grieving process? Will they feel they have to compensate in some way for the one who is gone? I know that I always find myself feeling sorry for the one who's left.

Whatever their reactions, there will be lessons involved, the trajectory of each family member's journey will be altered, and for each of them a significant learning curve will certainly result from the death of that child.

Sometimes it seems that nothing will bring closure to a parent's grief except the actual replacement of the child who is gone. I talked in the second chapter about the woman who discovered only after she gave birth to twins that her own mother had also had a set of twins who had died. And I said that she believed her own twins had been born to replace those who were lost and to help her mother come to terms with the grief she had never been able to acknowledge, much less overcome.

It's not unusual for parents who have lost a child to tell me they believe that another child, born after the death of the first, is their lost one returned to them. I personally know a woman whose daughter was killed in a car accident at the age of 17. She'd been the woman's firstborn, when she herself was only 17. In effect, they'd grown up together, and their bond was very close. This was, for her, a truly tragic loss even though there were also two sons born of her first marriage.

This woman was subsequently divorced. She remarried and had another son with her second husband, at which point she was told that if she bore any more children she would surely die in childbirth. Nevertheless, she went on to have another daughter, who she is now firmly convinced was her firstborn returned to her—a gift. And it was only after bearing that second daughter—at great risk to her own life— that she was able to feel at peace. She sensed that this was meant to happen, that the circle had been closed, and that she could finally come to terms with not having any more children.

I believe each soul has ways of "knowing" that are beyond the capacities of the conscious mind, and I know the laws of karma ensure that what we receive is in keeping with what we have given. And so, perhaps, if we have completed the learning a loss was meant to teach, we will "receive" whatever it is our soul most needs—even to the replacement of that which we have lost.

To lose a child will always produce radical changes in the way we live. It creates a new dynamic between parents, between parents and their remaining children, and between the entire surviving family and anyone who comes within their circle. It creates a hard grieving task that can be significantly affected by knowing we are still connected to the child who has passed. And it is possibly the most dramatic "signal" anyone can receive about the Program his or her soul has chosen to follow.

If you think that no one would ever choose to come into this world as someone who would have to suffer the loss of a child, please understand that you *did* choose the circumstances of your birth, your child chose *you* to be his or her parents, and that there were reasons for both those choices that your soul will understand, even if you, consciously, cannot. It all has happened for a reason.

chapter ten

spouses, friends, and also pets

We all need to find love in our lives, whether it's with the family we chose to be born into or through the relationships we form during our journey in this life. Once we've grown up and start to move away from our birth family, or when our family is no longer with us on this plane, we begin to create other families, both literal and metaphorical, of our own. The reason is because we need that sort of connection and interaction for the evolution of our Soul Program.

Certainly a spouse, and the children we might have with that spouse, become our literal, nuclear, closest loving relationships as adults. But, particularly in the modern world, where so many of us move far from home and do not necessarily marry or remain married throughout our lives, friends can be even closer and more loving than flesh and blood relatives, and can become "like family" for an enormous number of people. And then there is also the love we give to and receive from our pets, which may be (and has been for me)the most unconditional, purest kind of love there is.

When we lose any one of these loving relationships, it affects our life's trajectory. We need to grieve and find closure for these losses just as surely as we do for the loss of a parent, a child, or a sibling.

losing a spouse

The kind of grief we experience when we lose a spouse depends, as it does in all loss, upon how and when that spouse passes.

If we've grown old together, our paths will have been joined for many years, possibly our entire adult life, and the loss of a life partner can be both disorienting and devastating. How often do we hear of the surviving partner in a lifelong marriage passing over shortly after his or her spouse? And how often do we then hear friends and relatives saying something like, "Ah well, after Joe died, she just didn't want to go on?" In those cases, I think, it's not only their physical lives that were joined but also their soul paths. That soul *needed* to follow his or her partner from this plane to the next. They may or may not remain together and return together to a new physical existence, but there was some kind of unfinished business between them that had to be completed between lives.

Sometimes, however, many years pass after one spouse dies and the other remains on this plane. The survivor may then have unanswered questions about whether he or she is still remembered, whether they'll ever be reunited, and whether the spouse who died first will still love the one whose physical body has grown old. Here's how one gentleman put it when he described what had happened at his reading with me:

> For days before my reading, I talked to my wife in meditation about my life as it had been after her death, and about all my fears for the future, as short as it may or may not be. My greatest fear was to know if we would really ever be together again, but I was also concerned because this beautiful lady had died at the age of 46 and I was now 64. Would the gap have serious consequences for our Afterlife existence? I cannot tell you how many times before the reading I asked her these three things:
>
> Did she still love me? Will we ever be together again? If so, when?
>
> I did receive energy validation from her during the reading, and that made me happy, even though all that was relayed to me was that she just wanted

me to be happy for my remaining time on earth. The reading continued for some time and what I had wanted to know was not revealed to me. Then, as the session came to an end and I was gathering up my belongings, Suzane had one more thing to say to me. She said, "Your wife wants you to know that she loves you and that you will be together very soon, but not tomorrow." The exact answers to my three questions! I'm now, as they say, "good to go." I need no further validation from the other side. I have renewed hope that my wife will always be at my side.

The interesting thing about this man was that he had come with someone and wasn't really sure he believed in all this talking to dead people stuff. I found out later, and by his experience explained here, that he was about to leave still not sure until the moment I came back and gave him the final message that was the answer to his three questions. There are many that must have the messages or communication only come the way they want it. Otherwise, they are not sure they believe, or are willing to believe. In some cases like the one above, the DP knew how her husband was and made the decision that if he needed this answered in only his way, she'd do that. They do love us, those DPs, and it is only more evidence they are willing to go to great lengths to help us out of their deep loving bond. That is the primary reason they stay connected.

But what about those who lose their spouses when both are very young—to accident, illness, or unexpected disaster? There's always a program and reason at work there, too, that will affect not only the life of the surviving spouse but of the entire family. It was, again, Lisa Beamer, wife of Todd Beamer, who died attempting to overcome the highjackers of Flight 93, who said, "Some people live their whole lives, long lives, without having left anything behind. My sons will be told their whole lives that their father was a hero, that he saved lives. It's a great legacy for a father to leave his children." Growing up without a father will certainly affect the lives of those sons, but they will also be learning a powerful lesson as a result of his death. Everything has a reason.

Not everyone who dies young is a hero, but everyone leaves a legacy in the form of the lessons his or her surviving spouse and children will take from that death. Think of the many young women who gave birth to children after their fathers had died at the World Trade Center, or the women whose husbands go off to war and never get to meet their children. Certainly those women's lives will be dramatically different from what they had expected, what they would have been if they had shared the raising of their children with a loving father. And what of the children? They, too, have been left a legacy—their lives were determined by death before they even began.

There's always a reason, even if it isn't always clear. Those women obviously lost something very important, but perhaps they'll become stronger and more independent because of it. Perhaps they'll find opportunities for growth they wouldn't have discovered if they'd had a man to rely on. The children, too, have chosen to be part of that single parent family. Perhaps they'll develop a sense of sympathy and caring their soul needed in order to grow. Perhaps the reason was that they needed to learn to deal with adversity. And perhaps they won't all learn whatever lesson it was their situation was intended to teach, in which case they will continue the learning process between lives, or maybe in the next.

But it's not always the young husband who dies. Young men also lose their wives—if not to war, then to accident or illness or even childbirth. Losing a spouse to sudden accident can really jolt the survivor into an awareness of his own vulnerability— something many young men would rather not think about too much. Or, watching a lovely young woman succumb to debilitating illness can awaken a compassion that might otherwise have lain dormant for years. There are also serious challenges to losing a wife in childbirth. Will the father blame that child for his or her mother's death, or will he cherish the child more as a wife's legacy? Will the child feel guilty for having caused his mother's death? Will he find a way to forgive himself for that guilt?

As always, our reactions to what happens to us as we follow the blueprint of our program will determine the ultimate path of our journey, and no two paths, despite similar circumstances, will ever be exactly the same.

All surviving spouses, however, need to know that their loved ones haven't really left them to fend for themselves without any help from the "upstairs team." Their love continues, which means their concern for the future happiness and success of their surviving spouses and children also continues. And, within the limits of The Boundary Program, they will continue to be involved in those lives. That's always true, whether they died very young or very old; after a long life together or one that was cut short; whether they died of illness, accident, or any other cause. And simply knowing that can go a long way to helping the survivor shoulder his or her burdens and move successfully through the rest of life on this plane.

Here's a story that touches my heart:

> My husband had a favorite jacket. It was loved so much by him that he literally wore it to pieces. After his death, around ten months later, I decided I wanted to have it fixed up and redone. It was a TV crew jacket from a series, so it's quite valuable memorabilia that I didn't want just anyone to fix up. I asked a wardrobe designer I knew if she had a seamstress who could fix it up. She promised it would look good as new by the time they were done with it.
>
> A couple of months passed and I had forgotten all about it.
>
> It is now January 13, 2002 and my son's second birthday was the next day. It would be his first birthday without his father. I was fine all that day and

even organized a birthday party for him. Lots of friends about the house, but by the end of the day I couldn't help but think there was a real important person missing from that party. His dad.

The next day, January 14, my son was officially two years old. I drove to work after dropping him off, and found myself thinking about the jacket. I thought, wouldn't it be nice to have that jacket back now and I could give it to him as a gift from his daddy. I shrugged it off and continued with my drive to work.

As I'm getting my coffee that morning, I hear someone call me from afar. I turn around and see the wardrobe designer walking towards me holding a garment bag. Of course, what she brings out of it is the jacket. Good as new. What a beautiful gift for my son from his father on this, his real birthday.

Just one validation can sometimes be enough to change the survivor's way of thinking about his or her loss. Here is what one client wrote of her séance experience:

I listened for quite a while then Suzane said, "there's a man here who is pointing to the top of his head . . . is it a bald spot or is he covering it with a hat, I don't know . . . but he's showing me the top of his head, I don't know why . . . who is Frank connected to?" I couldn't believe it, my husband, Frank, had had brain surgery before he died that left a huge scar on the top back of his head. The brain surgery was the beginning of the end for him. She said more, too, but those words I have been playing over and over (I taped it). I'm still in shock, and every time I hear "Who is Frank connected to," I get this feeling that I can't describe. But, it's a good feeling, and since Frank passed, I haven't had too many of those.

Recently, one widow explained how much it had meant to her to receive a message of love from her husband:

During my private reading with Suzane, she contacted my husband and described his easygoing personality. She described our good, albeit short life together. She saw him wearing a blue uniform (he was a pilot). He told her I was due some money from his passing (I receive monthly benefits from his retirement fund that I hadn't known about before his passing). He told her he was responsible for sending a multitude of friends and people to help me cope; that I had stayed very busy and was never home. She saw I had moved recently, and he was happy about that. She described accurately how he had been sick, then better for a while, then relapsed badly, and how the last time he was scared and knew he would not leave the hospital. She spoke of a special ring with a stone—not a diamond or wedding ring (He had just given me a blue topaz ring).

Before that reading, I had gone to a group meeting. Each of us picked the name of a person someone else wanted to contact out of a hat. One woman picked my husband's name and without hesitation explained that he had contacted her, saying his wife was there and had taken his death

very hard. He professed love for me—the one thing I
needed desperately to hear.

I think it's important to note that the first message this woman got from her husband was simply
that he still loved her, and that she herself acknowledged that this was the most important thing she
needed to hear. But for me, her learning in our private reading that he'd had a hand in sending her a
"support team" to help with her grieving task is
again validation of the fact that the DPs not only
continue to love us, they also remain actively
involved in our lives. And again, I want to emphasize
how important that kind of support can be for those
who are grieving.

When an older person is left a widow or widower,
many of his or her friends may already have passed,
and grown children, although they may be concerned,
often live far away. But when a younger spouse dies,
the isolation that follows can be just as great. Couples
in the circle of the one who's gone don't want or know
how to interact with a single survivor. And women
often seem to fear that a young widow (like the proverbial "gay divorcee") will be on the lookout for another
husband—just possibly their own. Since it's most often
the women who are in charge of a couple's social
engagements, the young widow is unfortunately likely
to find herself left out of their plans. For some reason
this seems much truer in the heterosexual world, as for
example, than it is in the gay community, which
appears naturally to rally round and support those

who've lost a partner. I suspect this may be because there's been so much loss as a group, they've developed a depth of compassion that doesn't seem to pertain in the world of more traditional relationships. I have also seen this "rally round" dynamic in place in other communities based on culture and ethnicity. It all depends on what has been set-up as to nurturing indicative of the particular populace.

In the case of my client, however, Frank's pension was helping with her practical, monetary needs, but he also made sure that she received help with her emotional needs. And he was happy that she was keeping busy and, apparently, learning to move on. Without her awareness of his continued love and guidance, she might not have been able to do that so successfully.

when we lose a friend

Giving and receiving love, feeling loved, knowing that there are people who truly care about us—those feelings are essential to everyone's life. To learn about love is one of the basic reasons we are here.

Sometimes we don't get love from the most traditional sources—parents, spouses, children. Some of us don't marry, we move far from home, we may never have children—and if that happens, we need to create a loving family however we can. We find friends with whom we bond very deeply and, effectively, become our extended family. Or, even if we do have a family, we might not be close enough to them—physically or emotionally—to share our deepest thoughts and truest feelings. Sometimes we share those things more easily with friends. Because of this closeness—a closeness we've *chosen*—the loss of a friend can leave as deep and wide a hole in our lives as the loss of a family member.

It still amazes me that so many people who come to readings, séances, seminars, and workshops seem so surprised when they're contacted by a friend—either in addition to or instead of—the particular family member they had predetermined they wanted to hear from. That's why I spend so much time in the beginning of every meeting warning my clients about the danger of developing "psychic amnesia" and urging them to be as open-minded as possible about who will come through. After all, when the telephone rings, we don't know who's on the other end (unless we have caller I.D., and even that doesn't always work). One woman learned that lesson much to her surprise and delight when she came to a group séance:

> "Who here owns a male energy wearing a long white coat and a stethoscope and goes by the name of Alan? He suddenly was out of here—heavy pain in the chest—a heart attack," Suzane said.
>
> I looked around and realized that no one was claiming this prize. Could it actually be for me? My mouth would not move, but eventually I heard words coming out, saying, "I think I own this person."

Suzane picked her head up and looked towards me but did not open her eyes. She cocked her head and started to tease me with a sarcastic tone and said, "Well! He said it is about time you spoke up."

I gave a weak laugh because I knew in my heart that I was connecting with someone I dearly loved and to whom I'd never had the opportunity to say goodbye. She continued to validate that we both worked in the medical field.

"He wants you to know that he is sorry he could not say goodbye. It all came unexpectedly." She then asked if I understood this. I replied, "Yes."

Her next statement bolted me to my seat. "You two used to have an ongoing debate while he was alive, correct?" I replied, "Correct." "Well, he wants you to know that you were right and he was wrong. Do you understand this? Of course you do." Suzane then leaned back into her chair and was quiet for about five seconds. She then smiled and said, "He is laughing. He wants you to know that." She asked if I had anything to say to him. I was not prepared for that question. I said, "Please tell him that I miss him and love him." She smiled and said, "You can do that yourself, but he is aware of it."

At that point, I felt that giving me a million dollars would have paled in comparison to what I just experienced. My friend Alan had died suddenly of a heart attack. I had spoken with him only two days before. We'd exchanged pleasantries about our weekend plans and I said I'd check in the following week. And then he was gone. No goodbye—just gone. I grieved terribly because we were like kindred spirits. Suzane had closed my wounds by bringing Alan through.

When we were finished, someone in the group turned to me and asked what debate my doctor friend and I had been engaged in. I looked straight at Suzane, who knowingly understood, and replied that the subject of our ongoing debate was, "Is there life after death?"

Sometimes a "friend" will touch our lives only briefly at a particularly important juncture and change the trajectory of our path. Once that connection is made, however, it will never be broken, no matter how much time intervenes, and the bond will last even beyond this life. I was privileged to validate that unbreakable connection to a client not too long ago.

When I was a teenager, I met a minister, Father G, who "spoke to my soul." I connected with him immediately. There was just something wonderful about his faith, about his spirituality. He counseled me briefly, but we were not of the same faith and circumstances drew me away from his church. Through the years, I thought of him many times, and when I heard that he had passed away in Connecticut, I immediately included him in my family "circle" of DPs and began talking to him, praying for him, and wondering if he knew how much he had meant to me. He had opened a door for me. Because of him, my "spiritual quest" began.

During the reading, Suzane brought through a "Connecticut connection." I don't have any connections in Connecticut, never have. When the connection began speaking to Suzane about the significance of his "dress," I began to suspect that it might be Father G. But I had my doubts, since we weren't related or close in life. When Suzane asked what was significant around the man's neck, I knew it had to be him. I told Suzane it was Father G's minister's collar. And when she asked if I had known this man at a significant point in my life, I knew without doubt that it was him. Suzane picked up the initial of his last name, and the fact that he was a heavy smoker. I was certain it was Father G, and very much comforted and pleased to realize that he now knows what he could not have known in life, that his kindness and spirit greatly influenced me and put me on a spiritual path.

I am grateful for the reading with Suzane. Other relatives also came through. The connection with my mother, and with other relatives, confirms the bond that exists between us here on earth and those who have crossed over. However, the fact that Father G— someone I was spiritually connected to rather than "officially" connected—came through and reached out to me is, in some ways, a greater confirmation of the bond that exists between the living and the dead.

A bond is a bond, whether it's "spiritual" or "official," whether it's with someone we see everyday or someone whose path crossed ours and then moved on. In the same way that family always remains family, whether or not they're on the physical plane, so too, do those, who are connected to us by means other than birth, remain connected from one life to the next. There is always a reason for that continuing connection.

I would like to take some time here to address a question that I am continually asked. I really guess it is more to give some written time to an assumption most people make about mediums, and in my case, one who talks to those on the other side who have passed over.

I grieve just as anyone.

I am not immune to it. None of us can expect to escape pain. No one is exempt.

And, I have a Soul Program just as everyone else.

No, I can't just go around talking to anyone—calling them up—on the other side when I feel like it. I, too, sometimes need some help and some signs. I also go through the same pain as you when someone close is lost. Anyway you look at it, no matter who you are, loss is loss. Let me tell you a personal story.

I had a friend that was probably one of the closest people I have ever been to that was not part of my immediate family. I had known this woman for 25 years and we had shared a bond that had crossed the confines of definition—beyond sister. She was married and had children. I met her initially when I went out to Long Island for a workshop and she was there with her nine-year-old son, who at that time was already writing stories and turning them in at school about out-of-body experiences. We soon bonded and I would go out to work with her and others. She would cook me dinner in exchange.

Over the 25 years of our friendship we obviously would share some of the most intimate stories of ourselves. I learned that she had become pregnant at 17 and was forced, at that time because of the stigma of an unwed mother, to give up her child. A boy. This was something she had never gotten over and finally at a point in her life, her daughter from this marriage convinced her to start a search to find him.

She placed a notice on an Internet Website in an effort to find him. And, she did find him. As it turned out, he was looking for her also. He had actually grown up in the neighborhood and for a time had been her newspaper delivery boy. What are the odds of that?

There came a point, just over a year ago, that she was having some pain in the lower region of her abdomen and said it was like being pregnant. I told her that she needed to have it checked immediately and she set an appointment. We went together and what they found was a large tumor that was cancerous. They were to operate right away. I couldn't be with her for the surgery because I was traveling, yet was in communication with her daily.

When I finally got back and went to see her, there was a tube coming out of every part of her body. I couldn't understand how anyone could manage that.

She slowly was able to return home and her sister came out to stay with her. The doctors had done all they could to address the tumor and my friend was so convinced that it was gone that she ended up convincing a lot of people around her that it was so. I was in and out of the city and her sister was remarkable how she stayed, refusing to leave her. I am sure this meant so much to my friend because she had not felt much loved throughout her life.

She died last summer of Ovarian Cancer. It broke my heart and still today I am trying to move into understanding and process the feeling of loss. I, like you, am trying to understand the reason. To know that she had to have a child so young then have him ripped away, right from the womb it seemed, then to have a hysterectomy, and then Ovarian Cancer seemed so sad. We only found out later that her mother's twin had died of the same thing.

As I move through this time of adjustment, it seems so strange not to be able to pick up the phone as I have done over the years. It is also strange not to find myself on my way out to her house on Long Island. For most of the past year I have been on tour. I yearned so much for my own connection and wondered when and how it might come. Even I didn't have a direct line it seemed.

I was in Hawaii last November for a conference and was driving down the road one afternoon just for a relaxing few hours. I carried with me a CD soundtrack that someone had given me for my birthday of the movie, *Cider House Rules*. I love the movie and the music, and as it played I was thinking about my friend.

Suddenly the CD started to slow down and then speed up. At one point, it stopped. I ejected it and put it back in. It wouldn't play the first few times and then started up again, without hesitation, continuing to finish out the musical piece to perfection. All of a sudden it hit me. Teacher, listen to what you teach! Here I was thinking of my friend and she was signaling me that she was there. The movie is about a boy and an orphanage. Just like her giving up her boy at birth. I pulled over to the side of the road and just let the tears roll down my cheeks as I said a grateful, "Thank You."

Since that time, I have continued the tour that is planned and booked by my publisher. Now, if your into thinking that coincidences are just God's way of being anonymous like I am, I have been booked in the city where her son's wife was giving birth to my friend's grandchild, I have been scheduled just one year after her death into the city where her ashes were scattered, I am presently at this writing in Kansas City where one brother lives, and my next stop is a city in Texas where the other brother lives.

I get the signs that are being given to me and I know she is around me. And, I will continue to work through my grieving process just like everyone else.

and what about pets?

I often get this question about pets. "Where are they?" My answer is that they are just "hanging out" in the same place as the human DPs. Quite often my seminars, workshops, and séances appear to be overrun with pets. Dogs seem to be the most frequent visitors, but cats and birds also make themselves known and sometimes seem to be running the show up there (as they probably did down here).

They can be extremely persistent and appear to know as well as "human" DPs when someone on this plane needs to hear from them. I remember a séance last winter at which three dogs showed up on one side of the room, only two of whom my clients could claim despite fairly specific identifying information, including the fact that the one who went unclaimed had suffered from urinary problems at the end. It wasn't until days later that the woman suddenly realized the unknown visitor had been her close friend's West Highland white terrier, who had passed a few months before of kidney failure. At that point, she hurriedly called to let her friend know her beloved Angie was now okay.

Animals are part of a *group soul*. Animals do have souls, but they don't "evolve" in the sense that a cat or dog will become human in its next life. Animals, like humans, will always remain part of their own soul species. So, if you think you want to "come back" as someone's pet poodle, forget about it.

Domesticated animals, however, particularly our well-loved and pampered pets, often remain with their human family on the other side, and because their lives are shorter than ours, they can sometimes come back as another animal of the same species to rejoin us on this plane—if that's what both the animal and the human to whom it's connected desire.

For many people, the loss of an animal companion can be as—or more—devastating than the loss of a human loved one, and the animal soul seems to understand that as well. Many of the occasions on which I've been able to connect a pet owner with his or her companion in spirit have been just as moving, if not more so, than the connections I've been able to make between human family members and friends.

Last October, my 17-year-old dog and best friend, Larry, crossed over. I was devastated. I began to use Suzane's meditation tapes on weekends. I started to "see" more in meditations and then I started to see Larry, first just his eyes, then he was there to greet me at every meditation. This was the reward for listening to Suzane: anyone can do this, pets do cross over, and it's all about love.

Last spring I signed up for a small workshop with Suzane. It was one of the greatest experiences in my life and has probably changed my life forever. Before I attended the workshop, I meditated and asked my family to bring my Larry through, to validate what I saw and how I saw them, that the Larry in meditation was "real."

I felt a little sheepish having put Larry's name on my piece of paper while others were hoping to hear from fathers, daughters, and tragically lost children. But Larry had saved my life ten years before, and he was my child.

The man in the group, who got Larry's name, said he felt a pain in his legs and heard "Ben." Suzane came through with more information including the fact that he was being brought through by a male (who I later found out was my main guide) and my mother-in-law, who had brought him over. She then went on to the next person before abruptly turning back to me. "Is it dark where you live, is your house dark?" she asked. I knew immediately what she meant: I see Larry every day in meditation in a little hatchway, like a tiny cave or a very large rabbit hutch. That was exactly what I needed to know. I couldn't have written this script! Then I blurted out, "I know the name now— it's Bear! Larry was Larry officially, but in the family, he was known by many nicknames—Lawrence, BooBoo, Bear.

So the man, who read my piece of paper, had his name after all. And Suzane brought through my mother-in-law who crossed over tragically one year after my husband and I were married. She had a special bond with Larry and often said he could "say" grandma, though she was deaf and legally blind her last several years. Her love for him and her family, me included, kept her in this world longer than her body wanted, and made her a prominent figure in our lives.

I could not have continued to have faith in what I was seeing in meditation if it hadn't been for Suzane. This workshop opened my eyes to a new world and life.

Validation upon validation: You *can* do it yourself. Your beloved animal in spirit *will* come through. Animals don't cross over alone any more than we humans do, and they will remain with their loved ones on the other side.

One sad consequence of their being animals and our being humans is that we sometimes have to make hard choices for our pets (just as we sometimes have to make hard choices for the humans we love). Doing that can make the grieving process even more difficult as we wonder if we did the right thing, if the animal "understood," and if he has forgiven us. It's hard to find reasoning at these times, yet I know it's there somewhere. When I can relieve those doubts, as I did for Joanne, who joined me and a group of my fellow professionals on a retreat in Barbados, I always feel blessed.

For as long as I can remember, we always had a dog in the house. Sometimes we would even invite the neighbor's dog over to stay. So when the time came to purchase my own home, the only natural thing to do was to get a dog.

I remember walking through a local flea market and seeing a woman with a litter of month-old keeshond puppies—tiny little creatures resembling stuffed bear cubs. The most adorable pups you could imagine, but one special pup stood out. As I picked her up I knew she would be coming home with me. I named her Chewie Bear.

The years went by and she outgrew her bear-like appearance but not her frisky personality. She was a fun-loving dog and always at my side. Over the years, she lovingly welcomed two more dogs into our home and shared her space with them.

When Chewie turned 13 she started showing signs of her age. Her right rear leg wouldn't support her any more and she was plagued with digestive troubles. A month after her fourteenth birthday, I couldn't stand to see her in pain any longer. I'd always prayed that when the time came, God would take her in her sleep. But it was not meant to be. As

I walked into the vet's office carrying Chewie I knew that I would have to stay with her until the very end. The doctor told me she would first give Chewie a sedative to calm her. I could feel her body relaxing in my arms as she gently started to snore. Through my tears I stroked her fur and told her everything would be alright. The next injection would be the one to ease her pain. And then she was gone. I held onto her and silently said my goodbye. For the next four days I cried until I made myself sick. How could Chewie ever forgive me?

A few months later, I saw on John Edward's Website that there would be a retreat in Barbados. It was just what the doctor ordered. I phoned my sister who had just lost her husband, so it didn't take much to convince her we should go.

I decided before we left home that there wasn't anyone from the other side who would want to contact me and I was just going to relax and support my sister. But deep down I was secretly hoping that someone would tell me if Chewie was okay.

My first group session was with John. Many animals showed up that night, including a pet horse, but no Chewie. When I asked John why, he said it was a "them" thing and that if anyone were to connect with my dog it probably would be Suzane. As it happened, my session with her was to be the last of the retreat.

I prepared myself for better or worse. Suzane walked around the room, strategically placing us in just the right seats. I was to sit directly to her right. It didn't take long before Suzane announced that she felt a medium-size dog with a lot of fur. She asked me if my dog was the one with the heart problem, and when I said it was I who had the problem, she replied, "Your dog says to take care of yourself." She then asked me if Chewie had been sick and if I had put her to sleep. When I answered yes, she told me, "She wants you to know that it is okay and that she understands." All of the heartache I'd carried with me for months was finally being lifted. I had never known if I did the right thing and felt guilty because of it. I left Suzane that night with a feeling of peace in my heart because I knew that Chewie was really there.

I still think about Chewie all the time and she has even visited me on occasion. Sometimes at night I can feel her lying by my feet on the bed. I know she is happy where she is and she is running around like a puppy once more.

At last my Chewie has come home.

love is where you find it

There's no one to say whom we should or shouldn't love, or where it's acceptable to get love. All love connections enhance and enrich our lives in some way or another. Whatever the love connection, it comes about for a reason. When we lose a loved one, we grieve, and no one should try to tell us for whom, when, or for how long we ought to mourn. To hear someone say, "Just get over it," or "It's time you moved on," has always raised the hair on the back of my neck. Grieving is such a personal journey.

However, we do need to learn from our grief. If we don't, we won't be able to grow. Our soul will remain mired in the past and whatever lesson we were meant to take from this life will have to be studied again in the next. The grief process *stretches* our souls. If we weren't meant to love deeply or experience loss, it wouldn't be here. There would be no reason for it. Our loved ones in spirit—whoever they are—know that, and they want to help us move on.

And so, we should always be open to accepting that love and guidance wherever we find it, whether it's from a spouse with whom we hope to be reunited, a friend who touched our life deeply, or an animal companion who gave us unconditional loyalty and love.

We are all born for love.
It is the principle of existence,
and its only end.

— BENJAMIN DISRAELI

in conclusion

Where there is free will, it follows that there must be free choice, and the first choice each of us makes, even before we arrive on this plane, is to choose our parents, which means that we are, in effect, choosing the path of our life. We would not have free will and free choice if there weren't some reason it all played in the evolution of our souls. Although it may not become completely clear to us while we are here on Earth, the path that we choose is determined by the lesson or learning experience our individual soul needs to complete before moving on to the next karmic level and continuing its ever-evolving journey. I hope you have learned a bit more about how the Soul Program is manifested in your life, how you can affect its outcome by the choices you make in dealing with your life experiences, and have come to accept just a little more, if not to a greater extent, that everything happens for a reason. Above all, I hope you have begun to see how encounters with death, and communications with your loved ones who have passed can clarify and deeply affect the trajectory of you soul's path here on Earth.

Because every death affects us differently, and because our relationship with the loved one who has passed helps to determine the kind of learning we will experience, I would like to think you are leaving this book with a bit more peace and understanding concerning death, the Afterlife, and the events that happen in your life. No death will leave us untouched or unchanged, but just how we are changed in each of these circumstances can be the most profound lesson of all.

Our loved ones in spirit—the DPs—are here to help us in whatever way they can. The reason is that their love does not cease just because they have passed over. Although they themselves have completed their life on this plane, they take time from their continuing journey to reach back and touch us from the world of spirit. Even if our relationships with them were difficult or turbulent while they were alive, their energy and love never die. It's not only their wish, but also their duty to let us know that they're okay and that we shouldn't allow their passing to prevent us from moving on with our own lives.

If you have not yet had that contact with your loved one from the other side, never fret, your time is coming. Communications from the world of Spirit are always more abstract, symbolic, and open to interpretation, and those who had difficulty expressing their feelings or clarifying their thoughts when they were alive, aren't suddenly going to become great communicators in death. But, they will communicate with you if that's what you need or desire—at some point, at some time. We, the living, can make it that much more difficult for them by effectively "turning a deaf ear" and refusing to listen to what they have to say simply because they're not saying it in exactly the way we think they should, or the way we've already decided we want to hear it.

I always urge people to try to resolve whatever problems they might have while their loved ones are still present. The people who come into our lives are always present for a reason—because they have something to teach us; because we have something to teach them; because our souls' journeys have taken similar trajectories—and we'd do well to try to learn those lessons in this lifetime rather than carrying them with us into the next. Unfortunately, that's not always possible. But I do know, with certainty, that whatever questions we might still have about the path our life has taken, there is a reason for that path and it *will* be answered when we cross to the next plane.

We are in a time of decision. Will we remain satisfied living in a space of denial and ignorance, and unresolved issues? This is a time that is calling each and every one of us to *step up to the plate* with a deep dedication to our loved ones, our relationships, our lives, and ourselves. We are called to learn how to live and speak our truth with love, compassion, understanding, and forgiveness. For others, and ourselves. We are excitingly on the threshold of the old and new, of light and dark, of illusion and truth, and adventure and complacency. I believe it is awesome! There can be no doubt there is a reason we find ourselves at the point we are in time. We have created it.

While I'm here, I consider that the powerful gift I've been given comes with a responsibility, which is to give love and live love on this plane. That's the essence of my work. I believe that the most important lesson we can learn from dealing with death *and* life is that we all have a responsibility to show care, compassion, and love. The DPs know this, and I hope that, having read this book, you, too, will better understand the power and peace that can derive from the undying energy of love, and that you also have come to a better understanding that everything happens for a reason.

about the author

SUZANE NORTHROP is a nationally recognized trance medium and expert in psychic phenomena. She discovered her "gift" as a young child, and for the past 25 years has been using that gift to help bridge the gap between the world of the living and the spirit world. Suzane brings a unique contribution to the ever-growing body of literature by and about those who communicate with souls who have passed over to another plane. Rather than simply relating stories gleaned from her work, she has made it her mission to convey her understanding that each of us is here on earth, in this lifetime, for a reason, and that reason is to complete a particular portion of what will be a never-ending journey of the soul.

In her first book for Jodere Group, *Second Chance: Healing Messages from the Afterlife*, Suzane shares her journey of discovery, acceptance, and guidance through life with the Dead Peoples Society; a term she lovingly calls DPs. Suzane has toured extensively in the United States and Great Britain offering lectures and seminars to groups of hundreds, including New York University's Anthropological Society, New York Women's Bar Association, the Spiritual Frontier Fellowship, and both the American and British Societies for Physical Research. She has helped thousands through her seminars and private séances contact loved ones who have passed, bringing relief and clarity to what lies beyond our time here on Earth.

In addition, Suzane has used her gift while acting as a consultant to various police departments in cities across the United States, including New York, Washington, D.C., and Los Angeles.

Suzane's amazing and accurate abilities have been showcased in numerous radio and television appearances, such as *Extra, Entertainment Tonight,* and *The Leeza Show.* Other appearances include specials on MSNBC, Fox Family Channel, *National Enquirer TV*, and The Discovery Channel. Suzane was also a participant in an HBO documentary, entitled *Life After Life*, in which research was conducted into the study of consciousness surviving physical death. Other accolades include acting as a consultant for Demi Moore in the movie *The Butcher's Wife* and hosting a pilot for cable television. Suzane is also an accomplished musician and composer.

You can learn more about Suzane Northrop and her upcoming events by visiting her Website at **www.suzanenorthrop.com.**

We hope this JODERE GROUP book
has benefited you in your quest
for personal, intellectual,
and spiritual growth.

JODERE GROUP is passionate
about bringing new and exciting books,
such as *Everything Happens for a Reason*,
to readers worldwide. Our company was created
as a unique publishing and multimedia avenue
for individuals whose mission it is to positively
impact the lives of others. We recognize the strength
of an original thought, a kind word and a selfless act—
and the power of the individuals who possess them.
We are committed to providing the support, passion,
and creativity necessary for these individuals
to achieve their goals and dreams.

JODERE GROUP is comprised of a dedicated
and creative group of people who strive to provide
the highest quality of books, audio programs,
online services, and live events to people who pursue
life-long learning. It is our personal and professional
commitment to embrace our authors, speakers,
and readers with helpfulness, respect,
and enthusiasm.

For more information
about our products, authors, or live events,
please call 800.569.1002
or visit us on the Web at
www.jodere.com

JODERE
GROUP